Thinking With The Wrong Head

Dwayne A. Jones

Order this book online at www.trafford.com
or email orders@trafford.com

Most Trafford titles are also available at major online book retailers.

Note for Librarians: A cataloguing record for this book is available from Library
and Archives Canada at www.collectionscanada.ca/amicus/index-e.html

Printed in Victoria, BC, Canada.

ISBN: 978-1-4120-0676-7

*We at Trafford believe that it is the responsibility of us all, as both individuals
and corporations, to make choices that are environmentally and socially sound.
You, in turn, are supporting this responsible conduct each time you purchase a
Trafford book, or make use of our publishing services. To find out how you are
helping, please visit www.trafford.com/responsiblepublishing.html*

*Our mission is to efficiently provide the world's finest, most comprehensive
book publishing service, enabling every author to experience success.
To find out how to publish your book, your way, and have it available
worldwide, visit us online at www.trafford.com*

Trafford rev. 6/24/2009

www.trafford.com

North America & international
toll-free: 1 888 232 4444 (USA & Canada)
phone: 250 383 6864 ♦ fax: 250 383 6804 ♦ email: info@trafford.com

Dedication

I dedicate this book to my wife, Melanie, and daughters Mikaila, Jasmyne, and Niya.

Special Thanks: I would like to thank Laura Jordan and Kecia Murray for their inspiration and motivation that encouraged me to pursue my dream of writing this book. Also, I thank others who encouraged me along the way.

I would like to thank members from my Chapel Three families at Wright-Patterson Air Force Base in Fairborn, Ohio, who encouraged me to accomplish my goal with a minimum of effort.

Thanks Be to God

Without God's imaginativeness and vehemence, it would have been impossible for me to successfully write this book. With God all things are possible.

Thank you to Brian Kinney [admin@livingwordediting.com]

Contents

Introduction

Jesus said to the people who believed in him, "You are truly my disciples if you keep obeying my teachings. And you will know the truth and the truth will set you free." ["Make you free," KJV] (John 8:31–32)

Many churches avoid sensual and controversial topics. How long will churches continue ignoring issues and letting the people suffer? Many church folks are drowning in the sea of neglect and abandonment while life rafts are at their feet. Christians are struggling with sexual desires, expression of true feelings, lustful temptation, ethical decision-making, and "he and she devils." If you are real with your feelings, you will concur with this book as I show that this world is suffering because religious leaders, teachers, educators, parents, and other Christians are suffocating millions of people with the pillow of deceit and half-truths. . . .

Churches should be concerned about people's main questions, such as, "What do I do when I am hungry for sex and the devil is the head gourmet chef?" "What do I do when I am feeling sensual and carnal minded?" "What do the men and women do?" The church is quick to tell people to pray and God will take care of their lustful temptations. Many people are ashamed and too embarrassed to pray, because they feel God does not love them when they keep falling in the same lustful traps. As pastors, ministers, and spiritual leaders, we need to take off the "prayer bandage" and suit up for surgery. We need to deal with those hidden issues.

Furthermore, there are consequences for everything we do, good and bad consequences. Sexual immorality can have consequences of disease, unwed pregnancy, emotional trauma, betrayal, hurt, deceit, and even death.

I have discovered that the devil will show you the pleasure, but not the pain. A few moments of pleasure can bring a lifetime of pain. This book is designed to help you think about your decisions before responding to lustful temptations. I hope it is a blessing to you, as much as it has been for me.

1

A MAN WHO THOUGHT WITH THE WRONG HEAD

But they that will be rich fall into temptation and a snare, and into many foolish and hurtful lusts, which drown men in destruction and perdition. (1 Timothy 6:9)

For as long as I can remember, I have sought after women. Some reasons for this are more clear-cut and easier to understand than others. Curiosity, physical attraction, **lust, raging hormones**, economic instability, low self-worth, and a lack of affection from my mother are just the tip of the iceberg. The rest of the iceberg is hidden below the surface, unseen by the unsuspecting eye.

It is said that curiosity killed the cat. In my case this is true. I have not suffered a physical death, but I die daily from an emotional mortality, a slow and painful death that eats away at the core of my conscience because **I struggle to free my mind** of impure thoughts.

Since the age of six, I have been curious about the opposite sex. I always wanted to smell, touch, and feel—and even pondered tasting females. Often, I played games of hide-and-seek with my neighbors in the housing projects. The females would hide, and it was my job to seek them out and make myself more familiar with them. Most of the time this familiarization process came about through sexual contact. Whether it was in a bedroom closet or outside in the hallways (that reeked of stale piss), I found ways to satisfy my curiosity. I even tried to engage in acts of sexual intercourse during those moments, but rubbing and grinding against another inexperienced partner only leads to chafed and irritated skin. At the time, I thought otherwise.

Physical attraction was also a catalyst in my seeking women. Let us face it, beautiful skin, long hair, breasts, and junk in the trunk attracted

1

me to women then and even now. Any man who denies this is fooling no one but himself. Oh, how sweet it is to have a woman who has beautiful eyes, skin, and hair, and a beautiful physique, but my mother said, **"The same thing that makes you happy, can make you sad."**

Sometimes love was confused with lust. I was so in love with the way she walked or the way she smiled or the way she kissed, etc. . . . especially in love with the way she touched me. In fact, nothing else mattered when I was with her. The whole world and problems around me disappeared when I was involved with her. If arguments arose, then we would solve them with a moment of intimacy. Nothing could separate or come between us. When you are in "lust," nothing else matters.

Raging hormones played a large part in seeking women. As my body transitioned from puberty on through adolescence, I continued seeking after women. Chemical reactions occurred in my body and made me aroused when looking at women. Sometimes arousal occurred for no reason at all. Scientists still do not have all the facts about how hormones work. Neither do I, but somehow being involved with women helped control the hormones, or so it seemed.

Being kicked out of the home at an early age caused physiological damage. Symptoms ranged from mild, hardly noticeable effects to severe dysfunction. I suffered from depression and a lack of self-worth. I didn't receive the proper love and nurturing that a child should get from his or her mother. My stepdad abused mom and me. As I became older, I didn't tolerate the beatings and began fighting back, so my stepdad kicked me out. That led to economic instability.

Since I was economically and emotionally unstable, I sought after a cure-all. Women became that cure-all. **Sex was my medicine.** Also, the women I was involved with supported me financially. There were times throughout high school when I was homeless; I spent the night with female classmates or girlfriends. Do not get it twisted; I never did anything to them out of malice. I provided a service and so did they. There were a few special girls I regretted having involved in my life of turmoil. I did love a selected few and cared about most of them. Yes, I did use women to a certain extent. As a homeless teen, I had no choice. I had to sneak around in their homes when their parents were sleeping to take a bath and sleep, or I could continue climbing the fence at the local public swimming pool (after hours) to take a bath, and slept in abandoned homes. I'm thankful I do not have to do this anymore. **I'm saved through the grace of my Lord and Savior Jesus Christ.**

There were many times I had more than one relationship. In fact, I can't remember a time I didn't (except since marriage). I cheated because of reasons mentioned before: instability and lack of self-worth, along with insecurities and a need for maternal love. **I didn't realize then that all I needed was Jesus.** I also cheated because of an unquenchable desire for sex and affection. If a female told me she didn't love me or didn't care, she could consider herself cheated on.

I never spent a considerable amount of money on dating or luring women into sex traps. Once or twice, I may have bought a burger and fries and a ticket to the dollar cinema. I used charm and my physique — they were all I had. They were all I needed; at least I was foolish enough to believe they were all I needed.

Many mistakes occurred because I chose to use the wrong head. One of the first mistakes I regret ever making was having premarital sex. Some may think this is not a big deal, but having sex in your teen year's leads to a host of other problems. **I used sex like a drug.** It felt so good, and it was one of the things that didn't require money. Whenever I had problems at home with my stepdad, such as being kicked out, I ran to seek shelter in the arms of a female. Problems at school and work were also eradicated by sex, or so it seemed. I began to live for those moments of intimacy. If I could not receive intimacy in one relationship, I sought after it in another, which would also bring about problems.

Using the wrong head became a common practice for me. I began cheating on my high school sweetheart. She was a really sweet person. When I didn't have money or a job, she gave me what little she had. She took many risks on my behalf. There were times she let me creep into her home for a meal, a good night's rest, shelter, and . . . well, you know. Her father never found out, but her older sister busted us.

One night, she knocked on the door of the bedroom, and I had to gather my clothes and quickly climb out the window. The knocking became more persistent. She pounded harder and harder until it was almost like police officers with search warrants. I jumped out the window in the nick of time.Through the blinds, I could see the two sisters talking, and could barely hear what was said. We weren't caught in the act, but her sister saw and heard compelling evidence that confirmed her suspicions. Big sister knew what was going on, but wasn't upset because she knew of my situation. To top it off, she gave my sweetheart a condom and told her to be safe. I thought to myself, what a cool big sister (good-looking too). I never asked why she let us off, but soon afterward she started letting her boyfriend creep in, too!

My high school sweetheart loved me dearly. I was her first love. So, why did I cheat on her? I was young, dumb, and full of problems. We began arguing because she had a suspicion that I was cheating. Plus, I was beginning to be too much of a drain financially and emotionally. Her father didn't care for me because I looked much older, more mature. Or, was it that he didn't want to let his baby girl go?

As my sweetheart and I began arguing, the intimacy began declining and so did my visitation privileges. We argued so much that it led to the point of her saying, "I do not love you, go elsewhere for loving." I was foolish enough to believe that, so I cheated.

It was not just the fact that I cheated that she couldn't handle. It was the fact that I impregnated the girl I cheated with. That's what hurt her most. How could I bring a child into this world, when I was barely supporting myself? **I was thinking with the wrong head.** The more I think about it, I wonder whether I was looking for an excuse to cheat or whether I really felt that I didn't have anywhere else to turn for love. She stayed with me for a while and tried to forgive me, but somehow word got back to her that I was cheating again. This time the word came from some jealous punk who wanted her, and succeeded. Later, they became engaged. They may be married now.

Using the wrong head didn't stop there. After my sweetheart left, I began a relationship with the girl I impregnated, a Hispanic girl with long, curly hair. I will call her Nina to protect her identity. Yes, I followed the same pattern of sleeping over at her home. Sometimes I would bounce from her house to my sweetheart's house.

4

Nina told me she could not get pregnant, and I believed her. How dumb could I be? Maybe I just didn't care whether or not she got pregnant. Like a farmer, I would plant seed after seed, and continued plowing and fertilizing her soil. Well, it is no wonder she became pregnant.

Her parents found out about me and everything was fine, as long as we were just friends. There was nothing wrong in their opinion with her being friends with someone black. But when she started showing signs of being pregnant and it was confirmed, they nearly lost it. Thus began the downfall of our relationship. Her mother said she saw me with another girl (my sweetheart) sitting on my lap, and she turned on me like a ferocious pit bull. We argued about it, and her mother used that as an excuse to keep me away from the house. They changed their phone number and wouldn't give it to me, only to my mother, because I was not allowed to call.

Separating us this way seemed to work. In fact, when my child was born, no one even told me. I just happened to stop by despite her parents' orders. I was heartbroken to see my daughter for the first time, two weeks after she had been born. As far as they were concerned, I was not her father. My name was not listed on the birth certificate. I had no paternal rights. I tried to establish paternity, but her family refused to cooperate and wouldn't sign any forms or documentation. I couldn't afford a lawyer — I barely had a roof over my head. Arguments for visitation rights led only to my being able to see my daughter for two hours on Saturdays — in their home. If I did not bring a gift for the baby, then I could not see her. Every Saturday I brought gifts. But some Saturdays I brought gifts and still wasn't able to see her. All I got were excuses about them not being home. No one would call ahead of time to warn me about them not being home. There were times I would knock on the door, and I could see someone peeking through the blinds, but no one would answer the door. Finally, I became sick and tired of the games. In a bag with diapers I left a note saying, "Thank you for calling to tell me that you were not going to be home." After hanging the bag on the screen door, I never returned to that house. I didn't call or write. I do love my child and pray for her daily. **Her mother would not accept my**

hand in marriage. What else could I do? I was thinking with the wrong head.

Moreover, if that wasn't enough drama in my life, I consulted with the wrong head again. I buried myself in deeper doo-doo. I impregnated another girl. This time I won't take all the blame. My college darling maintains to this day that she did not try to trap me, but I sometimes think differently. I cheated on my sweetheart with her also. To make a long story short, she didn't get off me when I told her to and . . . I now have my pride and joy, a baby girl.

I had a spiritual background while involved in sexual activity, but it was not strongly rooted. I used to pray with a couple of girlfriends before going to sleep at night.

My life was changed, when I "truly" became saved. I had been saved since my early youth but did not fully understand what it meant. Once I became married, I tried hard to live a Christian life. **Sometimes I fell, but I got right back up and tried to do better.**

The tree (below) shows us the roots and branches that indicate hidden issues which become problematic concerns. The roots represent what is underneath, the deep-seated stuff that is never resolved. Roots are the center and foundation of every decision we make. Therefore, if you have issues of unresolved pain, abandonment, anger, guilt, shame, depression, or incest, it is prudent that you seek immediate counseling and pastoral care.

The branches represent the effects from the roots. Sometimes you do not understand why you are doing what you do. For example: A man is abusive to his wife because he saw his father abuse (physical or verbally) his mother.

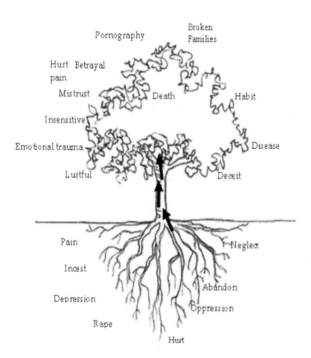

2

NO ONE IS EXEMPT FROM TEMPTATION

Stay alert! Watch out for your great enemy, the devil. He prowls around like a roaring lion, looking for someone to devour. Stand firm against him, and be strong in your faith. Remember that your Christian brothers and sisters all over the world are going through the same kind of suffering you are. (1Peter 5:8–9)

First, I want to show you that the devil does not discriminate against color, social status, creed, or nationality. Here are some quotes taken from several news media:

CHICAGO, Illinois (CNN) — Family and friends of the Rev. Jesse Jackson are seeking prayers and privacy for the civil rights activist and CNN talk show host after he acknowledged Thursday that he had an extramarital affair that resulted in the birth of a daughter now 20 months old. "I fully accept responsibility, and I am truly sorry for my actions," Jackson, 59, said in a written statement.

DECATUR, Ga. — The 80-year-old leader of a suburban Atlanta megachurch is at the center of a sex scandal of biblical dimensions: He slept with his brother's wife and fathered a child by her.
Members of Archbishop Earl Paulk's family stood at the pulpit of the Cathedral of the Holy Spirit at Chapel Hill Harvester Church a few Sundays ago and revealed the secret exposed by a recent court-ordered paternity test.
In truth, this is not the first — or even the second — sex scandal to engulf Paulk and the independent, charismatic church. But this time, he could be in trouble with the law for lying under oath about the affair.

Often we read or hear about a new case of sexual misconduct within the Roman Catholic clergy.

During his homily at St. Patrick's Cathedral on Palm Sunday, March 24, 2002, New York Cardinal Edward Egan called for a "purification of our church." Talking about the sexual abuse scandal of priests, the Cardinal said, "It is a time of great suffering for the church. . . . The cry that comes from all of our hearts is that we never want to even think that such a horror may be visited upon any of our young people, their parents or their loved ones . . . ."

The Catholic clergy in the U.S. as of today, June 14, 2002, CBS News correspondent Bob McNamara reports:

At least 300 lawsuits alleging clergy sex abuse have been filed in 16 states.

- Nearly 250 priests have resigned or been suspended.
- Four bishops have resigned.
- One priest was murdered by an alleged victim.
- At least two priests committed suicide after being accused of abuse.

It is becoming too difficult to keep track of all the Republican sex scandals these days. The latest "moral values" offender is Reverend Ted Haggard, head of the 14,000-member New Life Church in Colorado Springs, Colo.

"Haggard resigned yesterday as president of the National Association of Evangelicals amid allegations that he paid for gay sex during a three-year tryst with a male escort and used drugs such as methamphetamines. According to the acting pastor of New Life, Haggard admitted that 'some of the accusations against him are true.' Today, Haggard told reporters that he bought meth, though never used it, and received a massage from the accuser."

Jamal-Harrison Bryant has filed for a "limited" divorce from his wife, and she, Gizzelle Bryant, has filed for an absolute divorce from him. Both filed on the same day. There is a lot in the Maryland court system related to Jamal-Harrison Bryant that I and others usually do not talk about. We try to help people see a pulpit pimp's bad doctrine and try not to speak about other matters unless they hit the news media. But this is on file with the courts and sure to hit the news in time. Really, many of us have held back on some (many) issues with Jamal-Harrison Bryant. (There is a pimp in the pulpit!)

Jimmy Swaggart, America's leading television evangelist, has resigned from his ministry after it was revealed he had been consorting with a prostitute.

"The president adamantly denies he ever had a relationship with Ms. Lewinsky, and she has confirmed the truth of that," said Bennett. This story seems ridiculous, and I frankly smell a rat.

President of the United States Bill Clinton was impeached by the House of Representatives on December 19, 1998, and acquitted by the Senate on February 12, 1999.

As you can see, the devil will show you the good times, but not the bad times. A few moments of pleasure can bring a lifetime of pain. For a few moments of pleasure, it is not worth losing my wife and children. Illicit pleasure is a thrill that will exterminate your character, economic status, and spiritual relationship with God.

There is nothing more embarrassing than seeing your picture on ABC, NBC, CBS, and CNN as an adulterer, or caught in a sex scandal. Can you imagine walking around town, in the malls, in stores, attending churches, working on the job—knowing that people are talking about you? What do you say? What do you tell your spouse? What do you tell your children? What do you tell all the people who trusted you and emulated your integrity? The devil will tell the people for you. The devil will start the forest fire, but will not bring the water.

I must confess, I have been hurt by women. But I have hurt women many more times than women have hurt me. Regardless of what popular opinion may say about men being emotionally detached from relationships, men do have feelings and emotional needs.

The devil will not show you the legal obligation that you will incur from your moment of indiscretion. I discovered a long time ago that a court's financial plan is one-sided — in women's favor. Child-support court is rarely fair or painless. Paying child support is the right thing to do! However, the court is under the impression that all fathers try to avoid paying child support. Here are the facts:

1. Some fathers work diligently to avoid paying child support. Furthermore, they have no intention of paying support.

2. There are fathers who do work diligently to pay child support, and those are the ones the court tries to take to the cleaners.

3. It has been brought to my attention that many mothers will receive thousands of dollars, and their children will see little of this. **Some mothers take trips, buy new cars, purchase gifts for boyfriends, and the list goes on. While the mother is spending the money on insignificant material things for herself, the children need new clothes, shoes, braces, and school supplies.**

4. I believe that most mothers spend the money on their children.

5. Jails and prisons are filled with fathers who should not be incarcerated, but are there because some angry mother became jealous when the father of her child or children did not marry her, and has some other woman or wife. So, to get back at him, she wants to break him financially. How do you break him? Raise child support.

6. Some mothers make every attempt to turn a child against the father because he is not helping her physically to raise the child.

7. It is hard on children when the mother is in one state and the father is in another state. When you become emotionally bonded with your child, it is painfully agonizing to be separated from that child. The devil does not show you that when you are engaging in unhealthy sexual activity.

8. Too many children do not know their fathers. I know women who are reluctant to tell their children who their fathers are because the father is a married man. Men, stop thinking with the wrong head; family is too important.

9.   I know fathers who have acute stress from unstable and unhealthy relationships.

10. The bottom line is that the devil wants you to think with the wrong head. Always remember that God has an abundant life for you. However, once you allow the devil to lure you into the chilly waters of devastation and destruction, you will find yourself drowning in the depths of sin and damnation.

3

PREACHERS LIKE PIE, TOO

Do not you realize that those who do wrong will not inherit the Kingdom of God? Do not fool yourselves. Those who indulge in sexual sin, or who worship idols, or commit adultery, or are male prostitutes, or practice homosexuality, or are thieves, or greedy people, or drunkards, or are abusive, or cheat people – none of these will inherit the Kingdom of God. (1 Corinthians 6:9–10)

When I say that preachers like pie, too, Jimmy Swaggart is the first person who comes to mind. Swaggart would seemingly set the pulpit on fire, causing lightning to flash and thunder to roar. He was a giant in the TV evangelist arena. However, Jimmy allowed temptation to get the best of him. Jimmy Swaggart was a powerful and dynamic preacher. He was leading thousands to Christ for salvation. Nevertheless, **even the best of the best can fall into temptation.** Jimmy had several sexual relationships with prostitutes. I am sure that when Jimmy walked past prostitutes, he looked at them and wondered what it would be like to be with one of them – or maybe he was just in a vulnerable state of mind. The spiritual battlefield of temptation is in the mind. The devil starts his battle in your mind. **Once you begin to think about a person in a sexual and lustful way, the devil has you on the ropes.**

Matthew 5:28: "But I say unto you, That whosoever looketh on a woman to lust after her hath committed adultery with her already in his heart" (KJV).

This is why God warns us about lusting after someone or something that is not ours. Preachers and brothers remember that the devil is in the pie business. Whatever flavor you like, the devil has your favorite. If your appetite is for big booties, the devil has a big booty girl on the shelf who will make you want to go to the basketball court because hers is so round. If your taste is for big breasts and pretty eyes, the devil has one on the shelf who will make you lose your mind and your soul.

James 1:14-15: "But every man is tempted, when he is drawn away of his own lust, and enticed. Then when lust hath conceived, it bringeth forth sin: and sin, when it is finished, bringeth forth death" (KJV).

If your flavor is crazy and freaky, the devil has ten on the shelf crazy enough to make your life a living hell. You get the point. Money was not a temptation for Jimmy Swaggart. Money, political schemes, powers, drugs, and alcohol do not tempt some preachers. Certain women could strip naked before some preachers, and those men of God would be able to say, "Put your clothes back on," and they would just walk away (Don't try this!). The devil knows the right woman to send your way. I do not like apple pie! I love some sweet potato pie. If the devil sent an apple pie type of woman my way, I would not be tempted, but a sweet potato pie woman is a different matter. The devil would send me a sweet potato pie type of woman, along with some butter pecan ice cream to seal the deal.

Let's hear from John Williams who has been in the ministry for 15 years. He is going to tell his story; he knows the devil is in the pie business.

I've been in ministry since the age of 14. In ministry, I have been blessed to travel the world. I have been blessed to help people with all sorts of problems, ranging from sickness to pure hurt. However, in my quest to fulfill my purpose, I recognized that I was helping all those people overcome their issues, and **I hadn't dealt with my own issues.** My chief issue, above all else, was women. As much as I tried to shake them, as much as I tried to ignore them, this was my struggle. I simply loved sex (sex addiction is as bad as drug addiction). I loved to have sex in the morning, at noon, in the evening and at night. There were times when I would have two or three women in one night. I would try to suppress my desires, but it seemed as if I just could not do it. This was a stronghold in my life. It further matriculated into cheating and lying. I struggled to be faithful to one woman. I always had a "main girl"; however, she knew nothing of my indiscretions. She knew I was good to her. I took care of her. I took her out, bought her clothes, and paid her rent. I was good. I was real good! As time progressed, I did more and more cheating. I had more and more women. I had more and more sex. This produced more and more lies, which produced more and more hypocrisy, which produced more and more confusion on my part. As time progressed, my popularity began to grow. I was one of the most popular young preachers in Chicago. Nevertheless, with the fame that came from preaching in megachurches, **I was struggling. I was hurting. I needed help.** Not only did I struggle with women, I struggled with pornography.

First Corinthians 10:13: "There hath no temptation taken you but such as is common to man: but God is faithful, who will not suffer you to be tempted above that ye are able; but will with the temptation also make a way to escape, that ye may be able to bear it" (KJV).

Every night before I went to bed, I felt as if I had to watch pornography. I loved the thrill that came with watching other people have sex. That was my life: preaching, school, and sex. What was most interesting to me was that my peers (other preachers) had the same issues. It was as if there were hidden codes. We all did it, and because we all did it, that made me feel that it was acceptable. Many notable pastors would have secret houses to meet their women, scheduled meetings in hotels (not for prayer meetings); they would have children out of wedlock, provide cars for their women, etc. You name it, and they had it! It was almost encouraging to me to see my peers do the same thing that I was doing. It made me feel as though there was nothing wrong with it. As long as we covered each other, we (preachers) would be safe. I felt invincible! No way was I going to be found out, and if I was going to be found out, no way would I have gotten into serious trouble. **Well, one day my luck ran out and I got my "main girl" pregnant.** I was exposed. Everyone knew I sinned. I do not think I have ever been more disgraced, embarrassed, ashamed, and humiliated. What was worse was that my peers didn't cover me. **They left me out to dry.** I had to deal with the wolves. My ministry suffered greatly. However, I did recover. I thought that marriage and a baby would help me rid myself of my "women problem," but it did not. In fact, it matriculated from fornication to adultery. The women did not stop chasing me because I had gotten married, they chased me harder! **The devil's job is to destroy marriages by any means necessary.** I had to deal constantly with beautiful women wanting to have sex with me.

Proverbs 11:22: "As a jewel of gold in a swine's snout, so is a fair woman which is without discretion" (KJV).

In all honesty, I have given in numerous times. I wondered why I had this issue. Here is the problem as I see it. The first factor is how society has dealt with men, especially with black men. Women are taught from the time they are children to preserve their bodies. They are always taught to keep themselves pure.

First Corinthians 6:19-20: "What? Know ye not that your body is the temple of the Holy Ghost which is in you, which ye have of God, and ye are not your own? For ye are bought with a price: therefore glorify God in your body, and in your spirit, which are God's" (KJV).

They were taught that sex should be reserved until marriage and not before. God forbid if a girl got pregnant out of wedlock; she was subject to ridicule, slander, and shame. **However, men are not taught that from childhood.** Think about it, men, were you ever taught to preserve yourself? Were you ever taught that your body was a temple? In fact, I would argue that most men were taught to chase after women (Get it, man!). We were encouraged by our peers. There was added pressure put on us to lose our virginity.

Growing up, a young man did not want to be known as a virgin. His "boys" would laugh at him to the point of scorn. Even if we were not having sex, we lied and said that we were—which brings me to my next point: most guys lie about having sex. Most men's first orgasm experience is masturbation. In high school we all did it. Masturbation planted those seeds in our heads that it was okay to sleep around. Sex made you a man back then, or at least we thought it did. I believe the reason I have struggled for so long with women (I am still struggling) is that it is hard to find a good woman. In fact, it is just as hard as finding a good man! What most women do not understand is that keeping your man happy will keep him content and focused on you (my opinion). When I started dating my soon-to-be wife, there was nothing that she would not do for me. She would cook, clean, and give me sex whenever I wanted it. But as time progressed and we got married, most of those things came to a screeching halt! All of a sudden, she was too tired, or she was not in the mood. She changed! To her credit, the cooking did not change, but everything else did. It was not just the sex or the type of sex that changed, but her attitude toward me. She used to be concerned if I was okay. When I got home from a long day of work, I knew I could count on a hug, bath water running, and a huge smile on her face. I knew I could count on her doing whatever it took to make me happy. But over time, her desire to please me changed. Her time became consumed with other things. Children came into the picture, her career came into the picture, other friends came into the picture, her desires came into the picture, other people's endeavors came into the picture, and I was left next to last on her list of priorities. She complained more and more, our sex life was dying, and our marriage was in turmoil. On the other hand, when I got home my initial desire was to please her and the kids. I took joy in knowing she didn't have to work because I took care of her. It was a pleasure knowing I was a good man. But what happened? What changed? One word — this one word is the main reason people are divorced today — and that word is resentment. In time, I became angry with my wife because I felt neglected and underappreciated. I did not mind caring for her, but I too wanted to be cared for. I wanted her to ask me how my day was; she never did, and my sexual desires for her diminished. We all must understand that for most people sex is not just a physical thing, it is also an emotional thing. It is truly hard to make passionate love to a person you do not like. In many marriages today, people are having sex instead of making passionate love. What's the difference? Sex is solely based on achieving an orgasm, and making love is totally based on feelings and affections (the total package). Trust me, there is a big difference. My wife and I stopped making love, we were just having sex. When my wife was upset with me, she would withdraw sex as a punishing tool.

First Corinthians 7:5: "Do not deprive each other except by mutual consent and for a time, so that you may devote yourselves to prayer.

Then come together again so that Satan will not tempt you because of your lack of self-control" (NIV).

As a result of these things a huge void developed. And you know what happens to voids? Someone else will fill them. Once again, ladies came into my life, and it was hard for me to turn them down. I was in a pensive state of mind; deep down inside, I wanted to be loved. My last problem was me. I needed to realize that while these other problems added fuel to the fire, it was me who ultimately had to put out the fire. In the end, I have to give an account for the things I did.

Hebrews 9:27: "And as it is appointed unto men once to die, but after this the judgment" (KJV).

It is said that most men think about three things: sex, finance, and recreation. How often do you think about the things of God? If you think about sex 60 percent of the time, you are a strong candidate for sexual corruption.

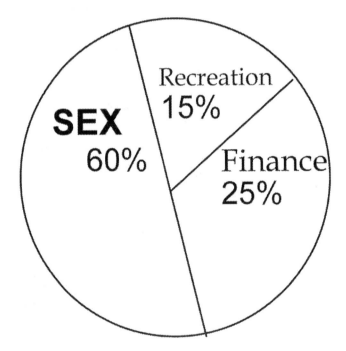

4

HOLDING SEX HOSTAGE

Give honor to marriage, and remain faithful to one another in marriage. God will surely judge people who are immoral and those who commit adultery. (Hebrews 13:4)

When I was a little boy, we had a dog named Dick. We would feed Dick table food. When I got old enough to do chores, my main chore was to make sure Dick was fed. Unfortunately, days went by without feeding Dick. After the third day, we got a call from our neighbors that Dick was eating their dog's food. Marriages are the same way; if you fail to feed your spouse sexually, he will go down to the neighbor's house to eat. Someone is saying, if he loves me, he will stay home. Tina Turner put it best in her song, "What's Love Got to Do with It?" I understand that men must have self-control, but self-control is out of control when it is obvious that you are withholding sex because you are upset or angry. Dick loved our family, but he was not getting fed at home, so he went down the street to eat. There is a myth flowing in the minds of many women, and that myth is, if you want to put your man in check, withdraw sex (lock down the pie factory) and he will straighten up and fly right. **I'm here to tell you that he will straighten up and fly over to another woman's bed**. Sex is a natural part of marriage; sex is a part of God's plan (within the institution of marriage). More importantly, if we deprive our spouses of sex, the devil will take advantage of the opportunity. You do not want it on your conscience that your spouse got caught in a sexual trap because he was weak, and you contributed to his weakness. No, you did not make him go out and cheat, but you contributed to his act of adultery by withholding sex.

19

First Corinthians 7:1–5: "Now about the questions you asked in your letter. Yes, it is good to live a celibate life. But because there is so much sexual immorality, each man should have his own wife, and each woman should have her own husband. The husband should not deprive his wife of sexual intimacy, which is her right as a married woman, nor should the wife deprive her husband. The wife gives authority over her body to her husband, and the husband also gives authority over his body to his wife. So do not deprive each other of sexual relations. The only exception to this rule would be the agreement of both husband and wife to refrain from sexual intimacy for a limited time, so they can give themselves more completely to prayer. Afterward they should come together again so that Satan won't be able to tempt them because of their lack of self-control."

I heard a female pastor tell a group of women that it is their responsibility to provide sex for their husbands even if they are angry with them. Her first point was that the only sex that their husbands could have legally was from them. Once you are married, you only have one sex source and that is your spouse. When that one source is cut off, where do you go? Her second point was that it is a moral responsibility to have sex with your spouse. Withdrawing sex is like playing with matches, and someone is going to get burnt. Someone will fall into a sex trap because he has a physiological need for service. Her third point was that holding sex hostage gives a stronghold to the devil. The devil is always looking for a way to destroy marriages. If a husband is craving for sex, the devil will prey on that craving.

God is going to hold you accountable for withholding sex from your husband. Talk out your differences and get back in the bedroom. Marriages are being destroyed because couples will not communicate and compromise on a robust solution. Instead, we choose to hurt that which we say we will love until death.

When you put the shackles on the pie, you might as well be working for the devil. **Every time you go on lockdown, the devil is rejoicing!** Take the shackles off the pie and stop holding sex hostage.

5

A RELATIONSHIP FROM A WOMAN'S POINT OF VIEW

By Angela Ward

In the same way, you wives must accept the authority of your husbands, even those who refuse to accept the Good News. Your godly lives will speak to them better than any words. They will be won over by watching your pure, godly behavior. Don't be concerned about the outward beauty that depends on fancy hairstyles, expensive jewelry, or beautiful clothes. You should be known for the beauty that comes from within, the unfading beauty of a gentle and quiet spirit, which is so precious to God. That is the way the holy women of old made themselves beautiful. They trusted God and accepted the authority of their husbands. For instance, Sarah obeyed her husband, Abraham, when she called him her master. You are her daughters when you do what is right without fear of what your husbands might do. (1 Peter 3:1–6)

A relationship can be extremely complex, but when it is broken, it is because some important elements and characteristics are missing. One of the elements of a healthy relationship is respect. A woman must first of all respect and love herself. Once a woman has found respect, she will set high standards. She will not settle for mediocre or run-of-the-mill man, and she will not look to someone else to determine her worth. Once a woman finds someone who respects her and treats her right, she must also respect her partner; in a relationship, respect should be mutual. In a healthy relationship, a partner's intention should be to lift your self-esteem, and not put you down. Words of affirmation and encouragement are what a partner should be giving, not negativity and criticism. Love is something that helps a relationship grow.

Effective listening skills help to keep a relationship together. Having someone there to talk to, comfort you, and truly listen to you will go a long way in filling any void in companionship. Miscommunication is the root of most problems in a relationship. When people thoroughly talk things through and honestly listen to one another, it can solve and prevent an assortment of problems and situations. Something that truly makes a woman feel connected and appreciated in a relationship is affection. True affection is that subtle touch or those glances that let a woman know she is someone special to you. When it comes to communication, having the ability to translate what your partner is trying to say or portray to you is extremely important. When a partner is trying to express something, and the listener is able to read between the lines and pick up on body language and signals unique to the other partner, it allows the message to come across clearly and without misinterpretation. On most occasions you and your partner view things similarly or relate to things on the same level of maturity, which galvanizes the relationship.

Trust must be mutually present in order to make the partners feel secure and confident in the relationship. Having a sense of trust allows a partner to open up, which gives a feeling of freedom and allows that partner to feel comfortable in depending on the other. Having this sense of freedom and trust is what helps develop true intimacy. This isn't something that can be faked. It is what separates making love from just having sex with someone. Intimacy shows a true connection and elevates the relationship to another level. Deep and strong feelings must be present for someone to feel and express intimacy. Intimacy is something that makes the person feel connected to you on an intense and secluded level. Consistency in your partner's behavior and in the growth of the relationship gives a sense of dependability. It is a wonderful feeling to be assured in your relationship, to have the luxury to look forward to the future and what it has in store.

To keep a sense of balance and fairness in the relationship, the situations and topics that arise should be negotiable. Being a part of a relationship is like being part of a team. It should never be a "my way or the highway" attitude. In order to keep balance and peace in your relationship, you must learn to negotiate, compromise, and meet on common ground. Once you have committed to a relationship it should no longer be only about you. Sharing your feelings, time, and material things allow you to show your partner that he or she is an important part of your life. Every relationship goes through trials and tribulations. A strong relationship should be able to endure hardships. Your marital bond should be tight enough that insignificant, common, or even drastic things can be worked out. They should not bring turmoil or destruction to the relationship.

When questioning whether you are in a healthy relationship, you should ask yourself, "Does this person make me feel incredible?" "Does he treat me like I'm his queen?" "Does he (or she) give me the utmost respect?" "Does she encourage me and compliment me as if I'm the most important thing in the world to her?" "Is he able to give me a future that I can look forward to, be happy in, and be proud of?" "Does she bring out the best in me?" In a relationship, there should be a sense of promise, a feeling of security and loyalty. You want to feel certain that this person will honor you and protect you. He or she wouldn't intentionally hurt you, and has your best interest in mind.

In order to be truly happy you must set standards. Your standards should be high and you should stick to them and do not settle for less. You should want someone who has the same strong moral values that you have.

I feel that all these elements and characteristics are what a healthy and successful relationship should contain. My perspective comes not only from a woman's point of view, but from experience and observation. Our perspectives and our decisions about relationships originate from childhood — the father and mother figure that we had growing up, or lack thereof.

Our concept of a healthy relationship isn't our own creation, but is taught, either negatively or positively. Our views on relationships are cultivated by various morals in society: those of your parents, grandparents, foster parents, friends, news media, and life experiences. The people with whom you spend the most time will have a strong negative or positive influence on the way you see relationships. Based on your relationships with friends and peers, you will frame a healthy or unhealthy relationship. Much will depend on the impact of any negative example in your life. If that's the case, sometimes you can subconsciously be attracted to or choose a person who is the exact opposite of what you want. I feel this choice stems from not knowing and owning your true net worth. If women could realize they are worth waiting for, they would achieve great things, and stop settling for less.

I can't stress enough that having high standards and knowing your self-worth are the two keys to choosing a partner who will produce a happy and successful relationship. No one deserves to be mistreated or unappreciated. This concept goes both ways because it takes two to be successful in a relationship. This concept is not to be taken lightly or misinterpreted.

If someone truly cares about you, he won't curse you, cheat on you, hit you, misuse your finances, mistreat you, and otherwise produce an unhealthy relationship.

When you consider entering a relationship, you should always look before you leap. That means you should research that person's childhood and background for how he was raised, the type of environment he came from, his relationship with his family, what types of people he considers friends, and his prior relationships. Sometimes people are hesitant to do these things because they do not want to feel like they are prejudging. Regardless of how we may want to deny our life experiences, the things we go through in life mold and shape the type of person we will become. How we were raised, our environment, and the different experiences we go through in life affect numerous things. They affect our view of a relationship, how we interact with people, how we deal with conflict, how we manage our finances, our work ethic, and many other things that you would eventually encounter once you get involved with the person. If you're trying to get seriously involved with someone, you need to go out of your way to discover who he truly is and whether he will be compatible with you. In order to make the right decision, you must first take the time and effort to find out who you are and what you want from a relationship.

I would like to take this opportunity to share my female point of view on "dog men" and talk about how most of them do not appreciate good women, or know how to treat them. If we want to change the pattern of unsuccessful and unhealthy relationships, the change must start with ourselves. If you want a "real man" stop serving dog food. When we ask men, "Do you love me…" in the middle of having sex, what do you think he is going to say? He is going to say, "Yes…you know I do…" the next day, don't get upset when he doesn't remember the conversation. Oh yeah, stop telling men, "This is your pie…" and, "You have a good peppermint stick…." Wake up! They don't want you; they want your pie. You are serving dog food; you are what you eat. You are turning men into nasty dogs.

This is coming from a woman who has experienced the good, the bad, and the ugly. We must first learn to appreciate, respect, and love ourselves. Then, we have to figure out what we truly want from a relationship. Once you have been through enough bad relationships, you will know what you do not want. Set your standards and do not stray from them. When it came to choosing the right man, I once was blind, but through trials, tribulations, and heartache, now I see. I now know what my first mistake was. I didn't obey and cater to the man who should have been number one in my life; that wonderful man's name is Jesus. If I would have put him first and obeyed his word, and allowed him to send me "Mr. Right," I would not have had to go through all the heartaches. When you allow Jesus to enter your heart and truly focus on him, and obey him, he will fill that void in your life. We make the mistake of trying to fill that void with someone else or with the things of this world. It is better that your eyes are opened now, than when you are filled with bitterness and resentment. As long as you have not given up, it is never too late to love yourself and to find the love that you deserve!

6

IF YOU WANT TO KNOW, ASK A HO

It will keep you from the immoral woman, from the smooth tongue of a promiscuous woman. Do not lust for her beauty. Do not let her coy glances seduce you. For a prostitute will bring you to poverty, but sleeping with another man's wife will cost you your life. (Proverbs 6:24–26)

Let them protect you from an affair with an immoral woman, from listening to the flattery of a promiscuous woman.
While I was at the window of my house, looking through the curtain, I saw some naive young men and one in particular who lacked common sense.
He was crossing the street near the house of an immoral woman, strolling down the path by her house.
It was at twilight, in the evening, as deep darkness fell.
The woman approached him, seductively dressed and sly of heart.
She was the brash, rebellious type, never content to stay at home.
She is often in the streets and markets, soliciting at every corner.
She threw her arms around him and kissed him, and with a brazen look she said, I've just made my peace offerings and fulfilled my vows. (Proverbs 7:5–14)

Now, I need all of the "holy-than-thou people" who are reading this chapter to relax and hear me out. I know that most women shiver when they hear the word "ho."

First, I am talking about a sophisticated woman who has a Ph.D. in menology (The study of men). This type of woman is like a chameleon; she can change to adapt to the environment. She can change her color, taste, hobbies, social status, language, desires, religions, and gods. Whatever it takes to conquer her victim, she will accomplish the task.

Ladies, when you scold and yell at your husband or significant other, thinking that you are telling him off, you are empowering the other woman to turn him on. **If you want to know, ask a "ho," means that there are some women who are lurking in the crevasses of darkness waiting for the right opportunity to lure your man into the cave of destruction.** This kind of woman will adapt to your man's interest. If your man likes sports, she will become the queen of sports. I know some women who take no interest in their men's jobs, hobbies, likes, and dislikes. If you will not spend time with your man, some other woman will.

I have seen husbands with beautiful wives, but they cheat with women who are just the opposite of their beautiful wives. You wonder why in the world a man would leave a beautiful wife for this Delilah. I know why! This "ho" knows what she is doing. She knows the right combination to your man's needs. Sometimes a man's needs supersede his heart. A man resonates with his needs more than with his heart. Hint: Men have basic needs for sexual intimacy, respect, financial stability, a listening ear, and affirmation. Don't get mad at the other woman; it would be prudent for you to find the combination to your man's needs. If you don't know, you better ask a "ho," because she has already sized up your man within 30 minutes of meeting him. You have been married to your husband for 15 years, and the only combination you know is 10 to the right and 5 to the left. You better put your ear to the lock and hear the click before that "ho" takes your peppermint stick.

Have an open relationship where you can talk about anything with your husband — men like to talk sex — if you don't, that "ho" will. A big mistake many Christian women make is not getting freaky in the bedroom. There is some freak in all of us. Your bedroom is not the place to be holy and pious. You are telling your husband, "No, I can't do that." Meanwhile, the "ho" is saying, "I do that and much more." She may be ugly and have no teeth, but she knows how to work her gums and have some fun.

Listening to Kurt Carr and Hezekiah Walker will not set an intimate setting for you to rock your husband's world and make his toes curl. You are walking around talking about how you don't listen to secular music; meanwhile, the other woman is playing some old school slow jams like Teddy Pendergrass, Luther Vandross, and the Isley Brothers, making your man's toes curl, and legs jerk. You may be angry with me, but I know what I am talking about. Most pastors and churches don't tell Christian women how to keep husbands happy sexually. I am telling you that this is not the cure-all, but it will heal many wounds. Some church members are in touch with what I am talking about. That is why they are walking around the church smiling from ear to ear between prayers because they are sexually content with their spouses.

Be vigilant in your relationship, and watch as well as listen to what your man is seeking in the relationship, and no "ho" will be able lure your man into any emotional death trap.

7

TEMPTATION: THE DEVIL IS A DIRTY PLAYER

Stop loving this evil world and all that it offers you, for when you love the world, you show that you do not have the love of the Father in you. For the world offers only the lust for physical pleasure, the lust for everything we see, and pride in our possessions. These are not from the Father. They are from this evil world. And this world is fading away, along with everything it craves. But if you do the will of God, you will live forever. (1 John 2:15–17)

The world is falling victim to the devil's tricks and schemes on a daily basis. We go to church on Sunday and worship for the devil during the week. We praise God on Sunday and raise hell on Monday. Meaning, many people are quick to give praise on Sunday, but slow to submit and live according to the Holy Scriptures. The church has become like a Burger King drive-through — we grab and go, but we do not grow. **The Word of God is not Burger King: We can't have it our way.** The devil is an adversary of Jesus Christ. The devil tried to trick Jesus in the wilderness as recorded in the Gospel of Luke, 4:1–13:

Then Jesus, full of the Holy Spirit, left the Jordan River. He was led by the Spirit to go out into the wilderness, where the Devil tempted him for forty days. He ate nothing all that time and was very hungry. Then the Devil said to him, "If you are the Son of God, change this stone into a loaf of bread."

But Jesus told him, "No! The Scriptures say, 'People need more than bread for their life.'" Then the Devil took him up and revealed to him all the kingdoms of the world in a moment of time. The Devil told him, "I will give you the glory of these kingdoms and authority over them — because they are mine to give to anyone I please. I will give it all to you if you will bow down and worship me."

Jesus replied, "The Scriptures say, 'You must worship the Lord your God; serve only him.' "

Then the Devil took him to Jerusalem, to the highest point of the Temple, and said, "If you are the Son of God, jump off! For the Scriptures say, 'He orders his angels to protect and guard you. And they will hold you with their hands to keep you from striking your foot on a stone.' "

Jesus responded, "The Scriptures also say, 'Do not test the Lord your God.' " When the Devil had finished tempting Jesus, he left him until the next opportunity came. (NLT)

The devil tried to tempt Jesus, but Jesus was full of the Spirit and led by the Spirit of God. When Jesus went in the wilderness, he was already full of the Spirit. He was prayed up, filled up, and led by the Spirit. Jesus had been fasting and praying, consistently in the presence of God. So often, when we go into the wilderness of life, we are not full of the Spirit of God. Therefore, we are helpless sheep before the BIG BAD WOLF (the devil). A prepared military soldier never goes into battle without his or her weapon. I remember one summer when we had a bad thunderstorm and the electricity went out. Everyone was looking for the flashlights — we had several flashlights in the house, but we failed to put them where we could find them during a storm. **We do the same thing in life; we struggle and yield to temptation because we wait until we are caught in the storm of life, and paralysis of poor judgment settles into our decision-making process, thus causing us to yield to temptation.** No one can fight the devil in a hand-to-hand combat. Charles Stanley, Benny Hinn, and T. D. Jakes cannot fight the devil toe-to-toe, or fist-to-fist. According to the apostle Paul; we need to put on the whole armor of God. Paul reminds us in the Epistle to the Ephesians 6:10–20:

"A final word: Be strong with the Lord's mighty power. Put on all of God's armor so that you will be able to stand firm against all strategies and tricks of the Devil. For we are not fighting against people made of flesh and blood, but against the evil rulers and authorities of the unseen world, against those mighty powers of darkness who rule this world, and against wicked spirits in the heavenly realm

"Use every piece of God's armor to resist the enemy in the time of evil, so that after the battle you will still be standing firm. Stand your ground, putting on the sturdy belt of truth and the body armor of God's righteousness. For shoes, put on the peace that comes from the Good News, so that you will be fully prepared. In every battle you will need faith as your shield to stop the fiery arrows aimed at you by Satan.

"Put on salvation as your helmet, and take the sword of the Spirit, which is the word of God. Pray at all times and on every occasion in the power of the Holy Spirit. Stay alert and be persistent in your prayers for all Christians everywhere. And pray for me, too. Ask God to give me the right words as I boldly explain God's secret plan that the Good News is for the Gentiles, too. I am in chains now for preaching this message as God's ambassador. But pray that I will keep on speaking boldly for him, as I should."

I can recall watching a movie titled *The Predator*. It was about a beast that turned invisible. It could see you, but you could not see it. A special agency sent its best commandoes to kill this beast, but it was difficult for the commandoes to kill what they could not see. The beast killed the commandoes one by one (except for one). It is much easier to kill that which you can see. . . . I say this because we are in a spiritual warfare; our fight is spiritual at first, then it evolves into a physical fight. The devil does not play fair. The devil does not play by any rules. Therefore, before you know what hit you, it is too late. The devil has stealth bombs that you cannot hear until they blow up in your face.

Readiness is the key. Any good football coach will study his opponent before a game. When I played football, the entire team had to watch and study films of the opposing team (our adversary). We had to study them! If we fail to learn about the devil—our adversary—we are going to lose something greater than a Friday night game, state championship, even greater than the Super Bowl. I am talking about losing your soul to the devil. The question that lies in wait is, who is the devil?

The Bible (King James Version) informs us that the devil is Lucifer (Isaiah 14:12–14) and Satan (Revelation 12:3–12), a serpent (2 Corinthians 11:3), the god of the world (2 Corinthians 4:4), the prince of this world

(John 12:31), the prince of the air (Ephesians 2:2), the accuser of our brethren (Revelation 12:10), the enemy (Matthew 13:39), and that wicked one (1 John 5:18).

As you can see, the devil is a multifaceted evil. The devil is not your friend; the devil is a dirty player. The Bible informs us that the devil is going to and fro, seeking victims to devour. Peter tells us: "Be careful! Watch out for attacks from the Devil, your great enemy. He prowls around like a roaring lion, looking for some victim to devour. Take a firm stand against him, and be strong in your faith."

Some people say to guard your heart from the devil. I say to guard your mind as well as your heart. The devil operates first in your mind. A person thinks about doing wrong before he actually commits the wrong. Nine times out of ten, lust is planted like a seed. For example, before leaving home, the mother tells her child not to take a cookie from the cookie jar. After the mother leaves, the child starts looking at the cookie jar and thinking there are too many cookies in the jar for his mom to know if he took a cookie. The child does not know that mommy counted the cookies before she left the house. Our fallacious and mendacious planning weakens our fight against temptation.

When the serpent was talking to Eve, he got into her mind. Every "player" knows that before you can get into a girl's panties, you must first get into her mind. I am not advocating that anyone try to get into a girl's panties. I am just saying . . . .

I am reminded of an interview that President Jimmy Carter had with Playboy magazine. In that interview, Carter said that while he had always been faithful to his wife Rosalynn, he had committed adultery in his heart many times.

Many who heard President Carter's comments thought that what he said was absolutely ludicrous. Adultery in the heart? Adultery in the mind? Jimmy Carter, being a conservative Baptist who knew his Scriptures pretty well, realized the heart of man was the seat of adultery and all sexual sins. He was very aware of Jesus' words in Matthew 15:19-20: "For from the heart come evil thoughts, murder, adultery, all other sexual immorality, theft, lying and slander."

It all begins in the mind; just thinking about doing wrong can make a person a strong candidate to sin. It does not make any difference whether you are married or unmarried. If our thoughts are impure, and coated with lustful desires, it is sin. If our thoughts are lustful, it is sin. I know the "holy church folks" do not want to hear that.

Many times, the thoughts start out innocent. You may see a beautiful woman, or a handsome guy, and you keep thinking about that person. Soon your thoughts go astray, thinking lustful things, fantasizing about him or her. You think about things that you should not be thinking about. James spoke about this in 1:14–15 (NIV) "Temptation comes from the lure of our own evil desires. These evil desires lead to evil actions, and evil actions lead to death."

Note: Temptation is not a sin; yielding to temptation is the sin.

TEMPTATION
- Temptation comes from Satan (Genesis 3:1–6)
- How to avoid temptation (Proverbs 7:1–5)
- How to respond when tempted (Matthew 4:1–11)
- God will provide a way of escape from every temptation (1 Corinthians 10:13)
- Run from temptation (2 Timothy 2:22)
- Christ can help us, for he, too, has faced temptation (Hebrews 4:15–16)
- God never tempts people to sin (James 1:13–15)
- "I know that in me (that is, in my flesh,) dwelleth no good thing: for to will is present with me; but how to perform that which is good I find not." (Romans 7:18)
- Temptation is defined as: (1.) Trial; a being put to the test. Thus God "tempted [Genesis 22:1; R.V., 'did prove'] Abraham"; and afflictions are said to tempt, i.e., to try, men (James 1:2, 12; compare Deuteronomy. 8:2), putting their faith and patience to the test.
- But: (2.) Ordinarily, however, the word means solicitation to that which is evil, and hence Satan is called "the tempter" (Matthew 4:3). Our Lord was in this way tempted in the wilderness. That

temptation was not internal, but by a real, active, subtle being. It was not self-sought. It was submitted to as an act of obedience on his part. "Christ was led, driven. An unseen personal force that bore him certain violence is implied in the words" (Matthew 4:1–11).

- The scene of the temptation of our Lord is generally supposed to have been the mountain of Quarantania (q.v.), "a high and precipitous wall of rock, 1,200 or 1,500 feet above the plain west of Jordan, near Jericho."
- Temptation is common to all (Daniel 12:10; Zechariah 13:9; Psalm 66:10; Luke 22:31, 40; Hebrews 11:17; James 1:12; 1 Peter 1:7; 4:12). We read of the temptation of Joseph (Genesis 39), of David (2 Samuel 24; 1 Chronicles. 21), Hezekiah (2 Chronicles 32:31), and Daniel (Daniel 6). So long as we are in this world we are exposed to temptations, and need ever to be on our watch against them.

Sin is not seeing or recognizing a beautiful man or woman. We see beautiful and handsome people every day. Sin is born from the continued thinking about a person; sin is when our minds run wild with scenarios of what it would be like to engage in sinful activities with that person.

Our thoughts can get us into so much trouble, because if we do not control our thoughts, they often become actions.

From the time we are confronted with temptation, we have that time until it reaches our mind, which is less than a sixteenth of a second, to decide what we are going to do. The question is, what are you going to do, or what decision are you going to make within that split second. Sigmund Freud verbalized three components that are at a constant struggle within our minds. They are the id, ego, and superego.

8

ID EGO SUPEREGO

And so, dear brothers and sisters, I plead with you to give your bodies to God because of all he has done for you. Let them be a living and holy sacrifice — the kind he will find acceptable. This is truly the way to worship him. Do not copy the behavior and customs of this world, but let God transform you into a new person by changing the way you think. Then you will learn to know God's will for you, which is good and pleasing and perfect. (Romans 12:1–2)

The Kendall and Norton-Ford book, *Clinical Psychology,* states: "The id represents instinctual needs and drives for sexual and aggressive gratification, operating on a 'pleasure principle' ("I can have whatever I want right now!") that is based on the 'primary processes' of fantasy and imagination rather than logic and fact."

Psychoanalytical theory states that the id is the part of the personality that contains our primitive impulses such as sex, anger, and hunger.

The id works in keeping with the pleasure principle, which demands immediate gratification. It is not concerned with self-control.

More times than not, we submit to the id. To the Christian believer the id represents sinful desires, the flesh, and the carnal mind. All of us have had some conflict with the id. There are times when we see a certain thing and think we have to have it. This is why 1 Peter encourages us: "Think clearly and exercise self-control. Look forward to the special blessings that will come to you at the return of Jesus Christ. Obey God because you are his children. Do not slip back into your old ways of doing evil; you didn't know any better then. But now you must be holy in everything you do, just as God who chose you to be his children is holy. For he himself has said, 'You must be holy because I am holy" (1 Peter 1:13-16, NLT).

There were times when I would see females, and I was already with them in the bedroom — mentally. I was thinking about them sexually. The id was telling me, "You know you want to, go ahead and get with her, do it, just do it." For years, I gave into the temptation, because I allowed the seed of lust to settle in my heart and spirit.

Every time I thought I had conquered this lustful spirit, I would slip right back into the hands of the devil. I wanted to do right, but my spirit was not renewed; therefore, I was still held hostage by the spirit of the flesh. It was until I read Romans 8:1-17:

So now there is no condemnation for those who belong to Christ Jesus. For the power of the life-giving Spirit has freed you through Christ Jesus from the power of sin that leads to death. The law of Moses could not save us, because of our sinful nature. But God put into effect a different plan to save us. He sent his own Son in a human body like ours, except that ours are sinful. God destroyed sin's control over us by giving his Son as a sacrifice for our sins. He did this so that the requirement of the law would be fully accomplished for us who no longer follow our sinful nature but instead follow the Spirit. Those who are dominated by the sinful nature think about sinful things, but those who are controlled by the Holy Spirit think about things that please the Spirit. If your sinful nature controls your mind, there is death. But if the Holy Spirit controls your mind, there is life and peace. For the sinful nature is always hostile to God. It never did obey God's laws, and it never will. That's why those who are still under the control of their sinful nature can never please God. But you are not controlled by your sinful nature. You are controlled by the Spirit if you have the Spirit of God living in you. (And remember that those who do not have the Spirit of Christ living in them are not Christians at all.) Since Christ lives within you, even though your body will die because of sin, your spirit is alive because you have been made right with God. The Spirit of God, who raised Jesus from the dead, lives in you. And just as he raised Christ from the dead, he will give life to your mortal body by this same Spirit living within you.

So, dear brothers and sisters, you have no obligation whatsoever to do what your sinful nature urges you to do. For if you keep on following it, you will perish. But if through the power of the Holy Spirit you turn from it and its evil deeds, you will live. For all who are led by the Spirit of God are children of God. So you should not be like cowering, fearful slaves. You should behave instead like God's very own children, adopted into his family — calling him "Father, dear Father." For his Holy Spirit speaks to us deep in our hearts and tells us that we are God's children. And since we are his children, we will share his treasures — for everything God gives to his Son, Christ, is ours, too. But if we are to share his glory, we must also share his suffering.

The "Ego": Should I Do It?

The ego is based on the reality principle. The ego understands that other people have needs and desires and that sometimes being impulsive or selfish can hurt us in the long run. The ego is a balance between rational and irrational reality.

The "Superego": Do the Right Thing

Gerald Corey states in his book, *Theory and Practice of Counseling and Psychotherapy,*that the superego is the juridical branch of the personality. It is a person's moral code, the main concern being whether action is good or bad, right or wrong. It represents the ideal, rather than the real, and strives not for pleasure but for perfection. It represents the traditional values and ideals of society as they are handed down from parents to children. It functions to inhibit the id impulses, to persuade the ego to substitute moralistic goals for realistic ones, and strive for perfection. The superego, then, as the internalization of the standards of parents and society, relates to psychological rewards and punishments. The rewards are feelings of pride and self-love; the punishments are feelings of guilt and inferiority.

We need to be aware that we are in mental as well as spiritual warfare. Regardless of what we think about, the battle is not too hard for God. We need to focus on heavenly things instead of earthly things. Colossians 3:1–6 states:

Since you have been raised to new life with Christ, set your sights on the realities of heaven, where Christ sits at God's right hand in the place of honor and power. Let heaven fill your thoughts. Do not think only about things down here on earth. For you died when Christ died, and your real life is hidden with Christ in God. And when Christ, who is your real life, is revealed to the whole world, you will share in all his glory.

So put to death the sinful, earthly things lurking within you. Have nothing to do with sexual sin, impurity, lust, and shameful desires. Do not be greedy for the good things of this life, for that is idolatry. God's terrible anger will come upon those who do such things.

9

BOUNDARIES: KNOWING YOUR LIMITS

And remember, no one who wants to do wrong should ever say, "God is tempting me." God is never tempted to do wrong and he never tempts anyone else either. Temptation comes from the lure of our own evil desires. (James 1:13–14 NLT)

In the book titled *Boundaries*, by Dr. Cloud and Dr. Townsend, we are told that boundaries define us — that boundaries define what is me and what is not me. A boundary shows the beginning and end of something. Boundaries state that you have limits, and within those limits you have a responsibility. Everyone should set boundaries. Setting boundaries is not easy for everyone. Therefore, we need a boundary checklist. I have adopted Cloud and Townsend's checklist to support my point:

1. What are the symptoms? Look at the destructive fruit you may be exhibiting by not being able to say no to yourself. You may be experiencing depression, anxiety, panic, phobias, rage, relationship struggles, isolation and work problems, or psychosomatic problems.

All of these symptoms can be related to a difficulty in setting limits on your own behavior. Use them as a road map to begin identifying the particular boundary problem you are having.

2. What are the roots? Identifying the causes of your self-boundary problems will assist you in understanding your own contribution to the problem (how you have sinned), your developmental injuries (how you have been sinned against), and the significant relationships that may have contributed to the problem.

Some people never learned to accept limits, to pay the consequences of their actions, or to delay self-gratification when they were growing up. For example, they may never have experienced any consequence for talking back as a child. Obedience to boundaries will protect you from unnecessary hardship down the road.

Let us focus our attention on 2 Samuel 11:

The following spring, the time of year when kings go to war, David sent Joab and the Israelite army to destroy the Ammonites. In the process they laid siege to the city of Rabbah. But David stayed behind in Jerusalem. Late one afternoon David got out of bed after taking a nap and went for a stroll on the roof of the palace. As he looked out over the city, he noticed a woman of unusual beauty taking a bath. He sent someone to find out who she was, and he was told, "She is Bathsheba, the daughter of Eliam and the wife of Uriah the Hittite." Then David sent for her; and when she came to the palace, he slept with her. (She had just completed the purification rites after having her menstrual period.) Then she returned home. Later, when Bathsheba discovered that she was pregnant, she sent a message to inform David. (2 Samuel 11:1–8)

King David overstepped his boundaries by sleeping with Uriah's wife. David was engrossed with Bathsheba's beauty and he failed to operate within his boundaries. Regardless of who you are, you have boundaries. President Clinton's affair with Monica Lewinski reminds me that we are never above God's Law . . . there are consequences for everything we do. President Clinton's position as president of the United States and marriage to Hilary should have been enough to put his boundaries in perspective. Nevertheless, the devil knows how to destroy great people in great positions. The devil is the master dog handler. A master dog handler knows how to get the best out of any dog. Contrary to popular opinion, there is a little dog in all of us. **The little "doggy" might be sleeping, but the right smell, sound, push, kick . . . will wake any dog.**

David was sleeping and woke up; he walked around on his rooftop and saw a beautiful woman bathing. David's "dog" woke up when he saw this beautiful woman bathing. David's inquiry about Bathsheba caused him to cross boundaries that lead to the death of his firstborn, and the death of Uriah, both innocent people. David sent some of his "homies" to check out Bathsheba. In order to meet someone, it is essential that you do some background investigation. David did what most men would do, that is, check out the goods. Have you ever seen a young lady to whom you were attracted, and you sent a friend to check her out for you? I understand part of David's thinking. However, when the report came back to David, he was told by the "home boys" that Bathsheba was married and her husband was one of his elite guards (David hand-picked Uriah as one of his personal bodyguards). What about David's loyalty and commitment to his elite soldier? Well, I tell you when it comes to self-gratification there is no loyalty. David was thinking with the wrong head. **David's boundaries were in his pants.** David's boundaries were disappearing and vanishing as he looked and inquired about Bathsheba. Sometimes you want something so badly; you do not care what the cost is. Nevertheless, there are consequences for everything that we do.

David knew! He knew! He knew what he was doing was wrong. He made a conscious decision to sleep with Bathsheba. It was a conscious decision by a God-ordained man who knew better. He was well-versed in the Mosaic Law. He knew the commandment said, "Thou shall not commit adultery." David's passion overwhelmed his principles.

Then it happened in the spring, at the time when kings go out to battle, that David sent Joab and his servants with him and all Israel, and they destroyed the sons of Ammon and besieged Rabbah. But David stayed at Jerusalem(2 Samuel 11:1).

David was lazy and lost sight of his purpose. He depended on Joab to do what God called him to do. God called David to be a leader and warrior. When God reveals to you your purpose, you cannot delegate your God-given purpose to someone else.

KNOWING YOUR PURPOSE

Myles Munroe states in his book, *In Pursuit of Purpose,* "Until purpose is discovered, existence has no meaning, for purpose is the source of fulfillment." A person without a purpose is like a ship without a sail. Many people are wandering around in the wilderness of emptiness because they do not know their purpose. Do you know your purpose in life? Not knowing your purpose is a dangerous thing. For example, if you do not know your purpose for your children, you will misuse them. If you do not know the purpose of your money you will misuse it. King David's purpose was to be a king for the people of Israel, but he decided to stay home. How would you feel if your king stayed home and you went out to fight? God consecrated David for a particular office and purpose. David was ordained to be a mighty warrior and king. When we fail to fulfill our purpose, we are planning for destruction and failure. When you know your purpose in life, you will become stronger and a more intensified leader.

If you do not know your purpose in your marriage or relationship, you will fail every time. If you do not have a focus, the devil will give you a focus and a purpose. You are created from the image of God; we are God's children. Ask God for your purpose, find your purpose, and focus on your purpose. You can do it. Do not think with the wrong head.

A THOUGHT FOR THE MOMENT

"Without purpose, life is an experiment or a haphazard journey that results in frustration, disappointment, and failure. Without purpose, life is subjective, or it is a trial-and-error game that is ruled by environmental influences and the circumstances of the moment. Likewise, in the absence of purpose, time has no meaning, energy has no reason, and life has no precision."

-Myles Monroe

10

Have mercy on me, O God,
because of your unfailing love.
Because of your great compassion,
blot out the stain of my sins.
    Wash me clean from my guilt.
Purify me from my sin.
    For I recognize my shameful deeds —
they haunt me day and night.
    Against you, and you alone, have I sinned;
I have done what is evil in your sight.
You will be proved right in what you say,
and your judgment against me is just.
    For I was born a sinner —
yes, from the moment my mother conceived me.
    But you desire honesty from the heart,
so you can teach me to be wise in my inmost being.
    Purify me from my sins, and I will be clean;
wash me, and I will be whiter than snow.
    Oh, give me back my joy again;
you have broken me —
now let me rejoice.
    Do not keep looking at my sins.
Remove the stain of my guilt.
    Create in me a clean heart, O God.
Renew a right spirit within me.
    Do not banish me from your presence,

and do not take your Holy Spirit from me.
    Restore to me again the joy of your salvation,
and make me willing to obey you.
    Then I will teach your ways to sinners,
and they will return to you.
    Forgive me for shedding blood, O God who saves;
then I will joyfully sing of your forgiveness.
    Unseal my lips, O Lord,
that I may praise you. (Psalm 51:1–15)

Years ago, my grandmother told me that moments of pleasure can bring a lifetime of pain. All of us have done some things in our past that make us wish we could turn back the hands of time. I have discovered that we cannot rehearse life, we must live it. I am sure Jesse Jackson wishes he could turn back the hands of time. Jesse has never been the same since the word became public that he fathered a child outside his marriage. In layman's terms, he cheated on his wife. Jesse was instrumental in advising President Clinton in his indiscretion. Jesse was a profound and articulate voice for millions of people. **Nevertheless, have you noticed how his affair (thinking with the wrong head) has immobilized and paralyzed his zeal, purpose, gifts, and talents?** Thinking with the wrong head can cost you more than embarrassment. I know Jesse wanted to turn back the hands of time, but he had to endure his consequences. There are consequences for everything that we do.

God loved David, but when David slept with Bathsheba he still had to face his consequences, the death of his firstborn son.

David had no excuse. Some men are always looking for an excuse to avoid doing God's work. My grandmother had a saying, "An idle mind is the devil's workshop." If David had been in battle fighting for his people, then he would have never caused Bathsheba to commit adultery, and his firstborn and Uriah would never have been killed. Sin has more power when you are in the wrong place messing with other people's stuff. Being in the wrong place and thinking with the wrong head stand at a juxtaposition that is a fine line of demarcation. When you are where God has predestined you to be, you can do anything but fail. God is not going to bless disobedience and laziness. David was called and set aside to be a king among kings.

Questions

1. Was David in the right place?

2. Where should have David been?

3. Are you where God would have you to be?

LOOKING CAN BE A TERRIBLE THING

Late one afternoon, after his midday rest, David got out of bed and was walking on the roof of the palace. As he looked out over the city, he noticed a woman of unusual beauty taking a bath. (2 Samuel 11:1)

Arterburn and Stoeker tell us in their book, *Every Man's Battle,* that we should set up our first defense perimeter with our eyes. The passage below is adopted from *Every Man's Battle:*

To set up your first defense perimeter with your eyes, you want to employ the strategies of bouncing your eyes and starving your eyes as well as the tactic of taking up a "sword" and a shield.

Let us first consider bouncing. You can win this battle by training your eyes to "bounce" away from sights of pretty women and sensual images. If you "bounce your eyes" for six weeks, you can win this war.

The problem is that your eyes have always bounced toward the sexual, and you have made no attempt to end this habit. To combat it, you need to build a reflex action by training your eyes to immediately bounce away from the sexual, like the jerk of your hand away from a hot stove.

Let's repeat that, for emphasis: When your eyes bounce toward a woman, they must bounce away immediately.

But why must the bounce be immediate? After all, you might argue that a glance isn't the same as lusting.

If we define "lusting" as staring open-mouthed until drool pools at your feet, then a glance isn't the same as lusting.

But if we define lusting as any look that creates that little chemical high, that little pop, then we have something a bit more difficult to measure. This chemical high happens more quickly than you realize, and drawing the line at "immediate" is clean and easy for the mind and eyes to understand. This "line in the sand" seems to work effectively.

"For God knows that in the day you eat of it your eyes will be opened and you will be like God, knowing good and evil. So when the woman saw that the tree was good for food, that it was pleasant to the eyes, and a tree desirable to make one wise, she took of its fruit and ate. She also gave to her husband with her, and he ate" (Genesis 3:5-6).

Today, sexuality is an area of struggle for a lot of people, and if you are in Christ, you must make this under subjection to your will, and let Christ show you how to control your body and to control those lustful emotions. That's the only way. The Bible calls it "sins of the flesh," and they are there at every stage of your life, just waiting to get the upper hand.

Lust, in contemporary usage, is a strong craving or desire, especially sexual desire. The King James and earlier English versions frequently used "lust" in the neutral sense of desire. This older English usage corresponded to the use of the underlying Hebrew and Greek terms, which could be used in a positive sense: of the desire of the righteous (Proverbs 10:24), of Christ's desire to eat the Passover with his disciples (Luke 22:15), or of Paul's desire to be with Christ (Philippians 1:23). Since "lust" has taken on the primary meaning of sexual desire, modern translations often replace the KJV's lust with a term with a different nuance. New Revised Standard Version, for example, uses crave/craving (Numbers 11:34; Psalm 78:18); covet (Romans 7:7); desire (Exodus 15:9; Proverbs 6:25; 1 Corinthians 10:6); long for (Revelation 18:14).

The unregenerate (pre-conversion) life is governed by deceitful lusts or desires (Ephesians 4:22; 2:3; Col. 3:5; Titus 2:12). Following conversion, such fleshly desires compete for control of the individual with spiritual desires (Galatians 5:16-17; 2 Timothy 2:22). First John 2:16-17 warns that desires of the flesh and eyes are not from God and will pass away with the sinful world. Here lust or desire includes not only sexual desire but also other vices such as materialism. James 1:14-15 warns that desire is the beginning of all sin, and results in death. Jesus warned that one who lusts has already sinned (Matthew 5:28). Part of God's judgment on sin is to give persons over to their own desires (Romans 1:24). Only the presence of the Holy Spirit in the life of the believer makes victory over sinful desires possible (Romans 8:1–2).

Deceit

1. Is falsehood. Psalm 119:118.

2. The tongue is its instrument. Romans 3:13.

3. It comes from the heart. Mark 7:22.

4. A characteristic of the heart. Jeremiah 17:9.

5. God abhors it. Psalm 5:6.

6. It is forbidden. Proverbs 24:28; 1 Peter 3:10.

7. Christ was perfectly free of it. Isaiah 53:9; 1 Peter 2:22.

11

DOING WRONG WHEN YOU KNOW THE RIGHT THING TO DO

When we are cheating in a relationship, we know what we're doing. The only real question is, what are we going to do about it? Let me introduce a young man whom I counseled several years ago (Dennis, age 29, married).

The interview went like this:

Jones: So, what brings you to my office?

Dennis: I cheated on my wife.

Jones: Tell me about it.

Dennis: Rev. Jones, I saw this fine girl, named Shantel, she was so beautiful. You just do not understand; she had a butt like a Spalding basketball. Her eyes were light brown; her skin was like caramel candy. Rev. Jones, you just do not understand. I would talk to her at work, and one thing led to another. . . .

Jones: What would you talk to her about?

Dennis: My wife and I were having problems, so I would talk to her about my wife. Shantel is a good listener; my wife never wanted to listen to me. The more Shantel talked, the more she made me feel special.

Jones: What do you mean by special?

Dennis: She built my self-esteem, gave me a sense of affirmation and respect.

Jones: What I hear you saying is that your wife did not fulfill those needs.

Dennis: True.

Jones: I hear what you are saying, but where is this relationship going?

Dennis: I do not know. . . .

Jones: How long have you been caught up in this relationship?

Dennis: Eight months.

Jones: How long have you been married?

Dennis: One year.

Jones: How did you get so caught up in this relationship?

Dennis: It started out with conversation, compliments, lunch, and it was on after that.

Jones: I hear what you are saying, but now is the time to end this relationship. This relationship is going to turn out ugly.

This session shows us that Dennis's primary need was emotional, not sexual. He needed someone to talk to, and someone to listen to him.

Thus, many affairs begin with innocent conversations and good intentions. I think when you talk to another woman about your wife, you are destined for a fall. Talking to another woman about your wife is an open door for adultery. If you play with fire, you will get burned. The grass may look greener on the other side, but you will find out that it is artificial grass...too late, you lost everything! Think with the right head.

12

According to the Feminist Women's Health Center, AIDS is the leading cause of death among African-American and Hispanic women ages 25–44 in the United States.

African-American and Hispanic women accounted for 76 percent of new AIDS cases among women reported in 1996 in the United States.

Women are one of the fastest-growing groups of new AIDS cases, accounting for 20 percent of newly reported cases in the United States and 42 percent of new cases worldwide.

Women are 33 percent more likely to die than men because treatment begins so much later, if at all.

What are Human Immunodeficiency Virus (HIV) and Acquired Immunodeficiency Syndrome (AIDS)?

HIV attacks the immune system so that, over time, the body has less and less ability to fight off infectious diseases.

AIDS damages a person's immune response so that the person's body cannot resist diseases.

There is a 4–6 month retardation period when the person becomes infected with HIV and when antibodies in the person's system can be detected by a blood test. Once a person becomes infected, he or she is an HIV carrier. He or she can infect another person at any time, even before testing positive. AIDS is a FATAL disease. There is NO cure!

People with HIV may look and feel healthy for 10 years or more. But, they must be on guard for common, everyday infections that can be deadly to them because of the HIV.

I knew this young lady (true story) who was an HIV carrier; she was beautiful, and stacked like a plate of buttermilk pancakes with a cherry on top. She was just as beautiful as Tyra Banks, and you know she is beautiful. I remember the guys running after this AIDS-infected woman trying to get her telephone number. Getting her number was not hard because she was having sex with every man in town. Of course, I turned it down. I was a probation and parole officer and knew about her case. She informed me that she was going to give the virus to as many men as possible because some man gave it to her and she gave it to her newborn daughter. Once again, because she was a beautiful woman, it would never cross your mind that she was infected. **AIDS does not discriminate; it comes in all shapes, colors, genders, and races.** How many people have slept with someone and did not know anything about the person's medical history. They just had to have it—AIDS.

God has a divine plan for our lives, and when we violate and transgress God's law and plan, there are consequences. Sometimes our indiscretion and consequences might kill an entire family.

In my hometown of Live Oak, Florida, I knew a woman who had AIDS; she slept with brothers, uncles, etc., and to date all of them are "graveyard dead."

If you are reading this book and having sex outside your marriage and/or with multiple partners, you are a strong candidate for contracting HIV and giving it to your spouse or significant other. If you do not care about yourself, think about them.

When you go outside marriage and have an affair, you bring diseases home with you. Brothers, we have to be careful and have self-control. There are some good women with good intentions, but there are some "she devils" waiting to inflict some revenge on you.

When you are thinking with the wrong head, you do not consider the consequences, but think only about the pleasure. The devil will show you the pleasure, but not the pain.

13

30 REASONS WHY MEN THINK WITH THE WRONG HEAD

So I say let the Holy Spirit guide your lives. Then you won't be doing what your sinful nature craves. The sinful nature wants to do evil, which is just the opposite of what the Spirit wants. And the Spirit gives us desires that are the opposite of what the sinful nature desires. These two forces are constantly fighting each other, so you are not free to carry out your good intentions. But when you are directed by the Spirit, you are not under obligation to the law of Moses. (Galatians 5:16–18)

(Most of this data is gathered from Infidelity Statistics) One should realize that suggestions may not be particularly popular, especially among men and women who are on the receiving end of the infidelity. Obviously, finding out that your spouse or partner has cheated on you is shocking and painful. Realizing that you are just another number that adds to the infidelity statistic is not something you would like to flaunt.

The reality is that there are a lot of unsatisfying and empty relationships out there. Infidelity statistics are high because people place a high value on their careers, children, friends, or hobbies, and not on relationships with their partners. Think about it, when you neglect any areas of a relationship, it is just a matter of time before they deteriorate toward an untimely death. The failure in the relationship becomes imminent. The bottom line is that if you want to avoid becoming yet another case that adds to the infidelity statistic, then you must nurture and prioritize your relationship with your spouse or partner. As you may have already figured out, unlike planes, relationships cannot be maintained on autopilot.

Recent studies (Infidelity Statistics) reveal that 45–55 percent of married women and 50–60 percent of married men engage in extramarital sex at some time or another during their relationship. Do these infidelity statistics seem a bit startling? What these findings suggest is that approximately one-half of all married men and women seek intimacy outside their committed relationships. But what does this really mean, and why are the numbers of men and women having extramarital affairs so high?

This may come as a complete surprise, but most extramarital affairs are not about sex. What then, is the main factor that causes infidelity? One should pay attention to the greatest reason that people find intimacy with someone outside marriage: because their emotional needs are not being met. This is true in most cases of infidelity that the partners want to feel emotionally connected to someone.

According to the current infidelity statistics, 60 percent of men and 40 percent of women are involved in extramarital affairs. These figures are even more drastic when the total numbers of marriages are considered. It is not likely that all the men and women having extramarital affairs are married to each other. At least half the women having affairs are married to men who are not included in the 60 percent of men having affairs — so at least one partner will have an affair in about 80 percent of all marriages. With this study, you can see that many marriages are affected.

The Jones Survey came up with the following answers as to why men cheat:

1. **They are conditioned by society**

Society is a large influence on what our young men think and do. Everywhere you look, sex is being promoted. (TV, internet, books, songs, etc.)

2. **They have no values**

Most people today are not teaching any values. Many homes do not teach values, Christian doctrine, self-worth, self-respect, and the view of the body as the temple of the Holy Spirit.

3. **They have no respect for women**

Lack of relationship with a mother can cause a man not to have an effective relationship with a female companion. An abusive female parent figure can cause resentment and a lack of respect for a female companion.

4. **They have no respect for self**

Many of our young men are so angry; they do not care about themselves or others.

5. **They see broken marriages in the home**

Young men see and emulate unhealthy marriages.

6. **They have no fear of God**

There was a time when most men went to church. Women had to go to church to find a man, but not today. Many of our young men do not attend church or Bible study. Our men do not pray like they use to do. I can recall when all of the men in the church would pray. Men just do not fear God. So, they are definitely not going to fear an unhealthy relationship with a woman.

7. **They aren't satisfied with what they have**

Society is conditioning our men not to be satisfied. People are not satisfied with their homes, always moving to another home. People are not satisfied with their faces, always doing something with their lips, hair, noses, eyes, etc. Even in the churches, people are not satisfied. Many people hop from church to church like Jesses James on and off a train. Men have learned not to be satisfied. Men find themselves looking for the greener grass on the other side of the fence.

8. **Their wives will not give them sex**

There are wives who think that they are punishing their spouses by withholding sex. I want you to know that you are pushing that man into the arms of another woman. Withholding sex has never been the answer nor will it ever be the answer. It is a control issue, not the solution.

9. **They need more than one woman**

Some men think they need more than one woman, but that is a fantasy. When a man feels that he needs more than one woman, it means he is a whoremonger.

10.   They have no boundaries

Some men are dogs. They will stick their peppermint stick into any jar. Some men have never had boundaries, so it is difficult for them to set boundaries — but not impossible.

11.   They never had a positive male role model

Unfortunately, our men are missing positive role models in their homes, schools, churches, and communities. It is difficult for a woman to raise a boy child.

12.   Their friends are cheating

I want to do what my friends are doing. They cheat! I can do it also. When friends cheat, it validates me cheating.

13.   They saw daddy do it

My daddy thinks with the wrong head all the time. He is a cheater and mom knows he is a cheater and she is not saying anything, so it must be okay. I want to be like my daddy.

14.   They were never prepared to combat temptation

Some men have no idea how to combat temptation. They think they are strong, only to find out that the devil is stronger. They fail to remember that if you play with matches, you will get burned. Men like to play with "pie," thinking they can overcome the temptation.

15.   They are afraid of commitment

This relationship is getting deeper than I want, so I am going to cheat to send a message that I want out.

16.   They are afraid of an intimate relationship

I do not want to engage in an intimate relationship.

17.   They do not think about the consequences

This is something that they want to do. They are not thinking about the wife and children. They are thinking with the wrong head. They have tunnel vision, thinking about self and self only.

18. They place themselves in vulnerable locations

If you are the mail carrier and you know that there is a woman who is always trying to get you into her house for a slice of pie, you need to flee. Men are naïve; they run to the pie instead of running from the pie.

19. They are thinking about the pleasure

Pleasure is the greatest sales representative in the world. The world is constantly looking for pleasure. Most men are addicts when it comes to sexual pleasure.

20. They look, and then they want

Looking catches men's attention; men are visual creatures. Once a man sees an enticing woman, he will start following her like a dog in heat. He has to have it, and he will not stop until he gets his woman.

21. They think that they won't get caught

Most men think they will never get caught. Some men have been thinking with the wrong head so long, the wrong head convinces them they will never get caught. The wrong head says, "Go ahead man, you have been doing it this long, one more time will not hurt."

22. They do not care about the consequences

After a person is wrapped up in sin, he does not care about the consequences. The wrong head says, "What is she going to do to you. You are the man!"

23. They do not respect the vows of marriage

One week after marriage, ask most men what the preacher said about the vows, and their response would be, "I do not know, I was thinking about the honeymoon."

24. They get caught up in the "whirlwind"

The "whirlwind" is constantly turning and looking for victims. Some men are not habitual offenders, but they get caught in the "whirlwind." These men are caught up in the moment.

25. They can't let go of masturbation

Men who cannot let go of masturbation stay in fantasyland, searching for the next high climactic ejaculation. They are enticed to women, hoping that one of the women will fulfill the expected fantasy that is embedded in their minds.

26. They don't trust women

Some men cheat because they assume that women cheat.

27. They want to get caught

If I get caught, it is an easy way out of the marriage. "Please catch me!"

28. Unresolved hurt from relationships

When a man brings baggage into a relationship, it is usually deep-seated. Many men act out their hurt by hurting others. Men can be very stubborn when dealing with their pain. Men do not like to take ownership of their hurt. We are taught to be tough and strong, not realizing that at that moment we are at our weakest.

29. They are addicted to sex

Some people are addicted to gambling, alcohol, food, shopping, drugs, etc. Some men are addicted to sex.

Men have reasons why they cheat. It may not be what you want to hear, but they have a reason. I am not justifying why men cheat; I am saying that they have a just reason in their own minds. Matter of fact, women have "just" reasons why they cheat. It is prudent to glean some understanding why your man is cheating.

30. Constant nagging

Sometimes because of constant nagging and quarrels at home, men will cheat. This might be simply to satisfy one's ego or to take revenge on one's wife or girlfriend. This deals with the emotional connection a man is not able to make with his wife or girlfriend, and that is why he goes out looking for a connection with someone else .

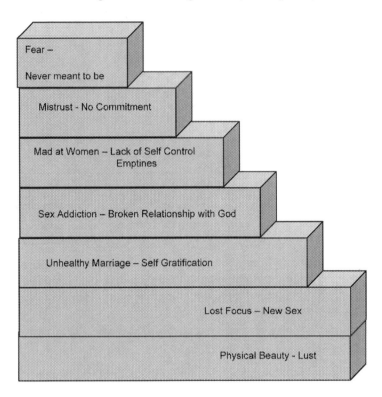

Steps Leading To A Fall

1. **Physical Beauty**: Men love physical beauty. Do not fool yourself. Just because she is beautiful does not mean that she is advantageous.

2. **Lost focus:** The idea of having sex with a new person is toxic to a marriage. New pie can make you lose focus on your God-given purpose. King David saw some new pie and he lost focus, lost a devoted warrior, and lost a newborn son.

3. **Self-gratification:** Lust will cause you to think about selfish needs. It is all about pleasure and not the pain.

4. **Broken relationship with God:** Sin will cause you to be intoxicated with sex and distant from God.

5.   **Emptiness:** Emptiness is when you are at a point where you do not care about anything or anyone. Your feelings are numb and void. You are cheating and you do not care if you get caught. There is no self-control.

6.   **No commitment:** Some people choose to show no commitment in a relationship because they want out. In this type of relationship, there is no optimism and no hope that the relationship is worth pursuing.

7.   **Never meant to be:** Some people marry for the wrong reason(s). Some marry for sex, stability, security, fear of being alone, to get out of the home. When you marry for the wrong reason(s), those false pretenses will surface somewhere down the road in the marriage. Some people are married and should not be married. Thousands of married couples are unhappy and desire to leave the marriage, but they feel obligated to stay for various reasons.

14

FROM TEENS' PERSPECTIVE

Why Do Teenagers Have Sex?
By Jade Noble

I do not believe that there is a fear of having or not having sex. The sexual act itself is hardly feared; the panic usually arises from the consequences of sex. However, there was a stigma surrounding intercourse that defined our antecedents' generations. Young women who engaged in sex were "sluts" or "whores." Young men were not reprimanded as much as their female counterparts for having premarital sex. Birth control and condoms were not easily available in America, so a one-night stand could easily result in a baby. Our young adults as well as our adults are having careless and free spirit sex. Unwed mothers are increasing. An illegitimate child often fragmented families who wished to maintain their "honor." The child often grew up destitute and ostracized for his or her parents' woes. The mother and father of the child were shunned from their communities or incessantly harassed. Examples of this come from the Bible, the Koran, the Torah, *The Scarlet Letter,* and *Tess of the d'Urbervilles.*

This stigma has tapered over the decades to a near end. We live in a country where women, blacks, youth, and gays have struggled for their rights. A new liberalism among American youths has surged. Anything is acceptable, including sex. **In fact, it is almost assumed that a couple in high school is sexually active.** A young man's friends often encourage him to "hit that," and a young woman's friends are accepting and supportive of her decision to "take the plunge." Mom and dad at home have become more lax as well. They are tolerant of their child's promiscuity and often buy condoms and birth control pills instead of persuading their child to remain celibate. A virgin in the senior year of high school is a rare discovery and grounds for being the butt of a few jokes.

The number of teenagers who have engaged in sex has decreased since the 1990s. In 1993, 56 percent of boys and 50 percent of girls in high school have had sexual intercourse. Ten years later, only 48 percent of high school boys and 45 percent of high school girls had engaged in sexual intercourse. The reason why has plagued the halls of academia and professionals alike for years. Is it because of the highly publicized effect of AIDS on sub-Saharan Africa? Is it because one out of four girls has an STD? On the other hand, is it because sex education has increased since the early 1990s and teenagers are simply more informed?

Yet another response is that teenagers realize sexual activity is overrated. Adults are more accepting of this behavior; sex is less controversial now. Sex has lost its "rebel factor" and is simply unimportant. Those who boast of having sex hardly receive congratulations. The response is disappointingly apathetic.

If I were to guess whether there was a fear (or fearlessness) of having sex, my answer would be no. So why do teenagers have sex? We have adopted a European stance on intercourse. It has become socially acceptable. There are no boundaries. With modern breakthroughs such as effective contraceptives and vaccines, there is a paucity of consequences as well. Teenagers will continue to have sex, at least in America, until another disease as tragic as AIDS reaches our shores. Then there will be a fear of sex.

Are Teenagers Afraid to Have Sex?
By Sharla Allen

I am 18 years old, and more than half of the people I hang around with have had sex or want to because they don't see sex as a big deal. Personally, I want to save myself for marriage. I cannot help but wonder why I am saving myself for marriage. Then I realize if I become married, I can give my all to the person that I choose to be with. I want to save myself, but at times, I feel like I am the only one. **When my friends hear I want to save myself, they think that I am being silly.** They say yes, I will save myself, but it will not be until marriage. They feel if the right person comes along, they will have sex.

Attending college is very difficult because the guys are very aggressive. Many of my friends are not concerned about moral values; sex has no significant value anymore. Most college students do not fear God; they do not care about Divine consequences. To say that teens have a fear about sex is asking a question that has many answers. Is sex scary because you can become pregnant or catch an infection that is incurable? Is sex scary because for a girl it will hurt? In college, the thought about pregnancy rarely comes to mind. I ask my friends what scares them about sex and the first thing that comes out of their mouth is that I think it will hurt. This is coming from the mouth of a girl. If I ask a guy what he fears about sex he will say nothing really it is just something that makes me feel good. The fears about sex are simple to answer. Intercourse is a fear and for most college students it is the only fear. Of course, students will wear condoms, but that is the only thing that they worry about.

One of the reasons for the rising feeling that there is nothing to fear about sex is television, music, and peer pressure. Mostly, the reason is peer pressure. There have been many times when I am with my friends and they start to talk about different experiences they have had with sex. **They tease me a little because they know that I am a virgin, but to someone else that gets teased it would make them want to go out and have sex because of the fact that they would feel less knowledgeable of what their friends were talking about.**

Another reason that some girls do not have fear of sex is because they want guys to like them. Some girls just want to make the guy happy because they are lonely. Another reason is some girls just like having sex. In this generation, sex is the norm. Below are quotes from some of my friends:

J'lia Boykins says:

"If you are a virgin then that is your choice, but if you are not, then that is your choice also Yes, I fear sex. She thinks that the fears of sex are STDs, pregnancy, HIV and AIDS."

Hodan Igal says:

"I believe you should save yourself for marriage, but if you happen to find that person that you have a connection with, then you should feel comfortable enough to have sex with them. Yes, I fear sex before marriage."

Marie Wagner says:

"Sex is very special and should be done with one person. At this time, yes I do fear sex. After marriage, I do not think that I will fear sex."

Do Teens Worry About Contracting AIDS?
By Janeshia Caldwell

Do teens even know what AIDS is? For most teens, they have learned or heard about AIDS whether from school or friends. Teens know that AIDS is a sexually transmitted disease and is contagious. They know there is a possibility of getting AIDS from having sex, but that is not their main concern. **In my opinion, teens are more concerned with pregnancy than catching an STD like AIDS.** They think that as long as they have protection, like a condom, they won't be exposed to those STDs. Some teens they think you can only catch an STD from having actual sexual intercourse. Teens think by having oral or anal sex they can avoid any possibility of catching STD or AIDS.

15

What happens after the vows are given, repeated, received, believed, etc.? What happens to couples between "I do" and "death do us part"? First let's review the vows:

> *Dearly beloved, we are gathered together here in the sight of God, and in the presence of these witnesses, to join together this man and this woman in holy matrimony, which is an honorable estate instituted by God in the time of man's innocency, signifying unto us the mystical union which exists between Christ and his church, which holy estates Christ adorned and beautified with his presence and the first miracle that he wrought at Cana of Galilee, and is commended of St. Paul to be honorable among all men and therefore not by any to be entered upon or taken in hand unadvisedly, but reverently, discreetly and in fear of God, into which holy estate these persons come now to be joined.*
>
> *I require and charge you both as you will answer at the dreadful day of judgment, when the secrets of all hearts shall be disclosed, that if either of you know any impediment why you may not be lawfully joined together in matrimony you do now confess it, for ye be well assured that so many are coupled together otherwise than God's word shall allow, are not joined together by God, neither is their matrimony lawful.*
>
> *Man/woman wilt thou have this woman to be thy wedded wife/husband, to live together after God's ordinance in the holy estate of matrimony? Wilt thou serve her, love her, honor and keep her in sickness, in health, and forsaking all others keep thee only unto her so long as you both shall live?*
>
> *I,_____, take thee,_____, to be my wedded_____, to have and to hold from this day forward, for better, for worse, for richer, for*

poorer, in sickness and in health, to love, to honor and cherish till death do us part, according to God's holy ordinance, and thereto I plight thee my faith.

With this ring I thee wed, and with my worldly goods I thee endow, in the name of the Father, and of the Son, and of the Holy Ghost.

Those whom God hath joined together, let no man put asunder. For as much as this man and woman have consented to live together in holy wedlock and have witnessed the same before God and this company, and thereto have pledged their faith to each other and have declared the same by joining hands, I pronounce that they are husband and wife together, in the name of the Father, and of the Son, and of the Holy Ghost. Amen

Effective communication

H. Norman Wright states in his book, *Communication: Key to your Marriage* , that God intended for marriage to grow through communication as two people share their lives together.

In time of war, the first thing the military does is to destroy the enemy's communication. If the enemy cannot communicate, they cannot plan and synchronize; they are facing defeat. They can have the best weapons, soldiers, and plans, but communication is the key.

I know marriages with great plans, a family vision, stable jobs, pillars in the community, etc, but due to the lack of effective communication, the plans are collecting dust, the vision for the family is on hold, and the job and community activities are individualized (no sharing).

The devil's primary job is to break down communication between married couples. He knows if they cannot effectively communicate, 90 percent of the battle is won. A couple can start their marriage with the best plans, endeavors, hopes, and aspirations, but if they cannot express themselves to one another, they are like sounding brass or a tinkling cymbal. Lack of communication in a marriage fosters a platform for divorce. Learn to communicate and your marriage will overcome all obstacles.

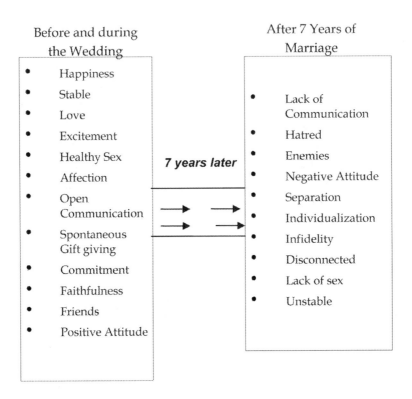

In the courting stage before marriage, couples exhibit open communication, spontaneous gift giving, and robust affection. However, when they become married, the lack of communication, individualism, and lack of sexual intimacy settles into the marriage. Note: this is not in every marriage; however, most marriages will experience some of the above.

The biblical standard for marriage is a monogamous relationship in which a man and a woman share a lifetime commitment to each other, second only to their commitment to God. It is an unconditional, lifetime commitment. Jesus emphasized God's intention that marriage be a lifetime commitment (Mark 10:5-9; Matthew 19:4-9). He affirmed this as the principle of marriage inherent in divine creation (Genesis 2:24). Paul cited this key principle to show the sinfulness of sexual relations outside marriage (1 Corinthians 6:12-20) and to emphasize the importance of self-giving love in marriage (Ephesians 5:28). Genesis 2:24 emphasizes the oneness of the marriage relationship and the priority of the relationship over all others, including the relationship of the couple to their parents. Marriage is also for companionship (Genesis 2:18–23). Paul described the kind of mutual submission that should characterize the marriage relationship (Ephesians 5:21–33). Although the husband is head of the home, his role is modeled after the role of Christ as Head of the church, who "loved the church and gave Himself for it" (Ephesians 5:25). The Bible says marriage is:

1. Divinely instituted. Genesis 2:24.

2. A covenant relationship. Malachi 2:4.

3. Designed for:

   a. The happiness of man. Genesis 2:18.

   b. Increasing the human population. Genesis 1:28; 9:1.

   c. Raising up godly seed. Malachi 2:15.

   d. Preventing fornication. 1 Corinthians 7:2.

4. An incentive in the early age to the expectation of the promised seed of the woman. Genesis 3:15; 4:1.

5. Lawful in all. 1 Corinthians 7:2, 28; 1 Timothy 5:14.

6. Honorable for all. Hebrews 13:4.

7. Should be only in the Lord. 1 Corinthians 7:39.

8. Expressed by:

   a. Joining together. Matthew 19:6.

   b. Making affinity. 1 Kings 3:1.

   c. Taking a wife. Exodus 2:1.

   d. Giving daughters to sons, and sons to daughters. Deuteronomy 7:3; Ezra 9:12.

9. Indissoluble during the joint lives of the parties. Matthew 19:6; Romans 7:2, 3; 1 Corinthians 7:39.

16

THINKING WITH THE RIGHT HEAD

Those who heard Jesus use this illustration didn't understand what he meant, so he explained it to them. "I assure you, I am the gate for the sheep," he said. "All others who came before me were thieves and robbers. But the true sheep did not listen to them. Yes, I am the gate. Those who come in through me will be saved. Wherever they go, they will find green pastures. The thief's purpose is to steal and kill and destroy. My purpose is to give life in all its fullness. (John 10:6–10)

In those days, when you were slaves of sin, you weren't concerned with doing what was right. And what was the result? It was not good, since now you are ashamed of the things you used to do, things that end in eternal doom. But now you are free from the power of sin and have become slaves of God. Now you do those things that lead to holiness and result in eternal life. For the wages of sin is death, but the free gift of God is eternal life through Christ Jesus our Lord. (Romans 6:20–23)

We make mistakes—no one is perfect. God is willing to forgive us for our mistakes. Some people make mistakes, but they learn from those mistakes. When we make the same mistake over and over again, it is not a mistake; it is a lifestyle. Do not get comfortable in your mistakes. A mistake is when you do something that you did not know was wrong, or when you were unaware of the outcome. When you sleep with someone and you are married, it is not a mistake. When you commit adultery the first time, we say it was a mistake—to be nice. Committing adultery is never a mistake because it takes intentional planning and a great deal of effort to carry out the act.

The great thing about life is that you can change at any moment. You can change today and think with the right head.

17

BUILDING A HEALTHY MARRIAGE

And further, submit to one another out of reverence for Christ. For wives, this means submit to your husbands as to the Lord. A husband is the head of his wife as Christ is the head of the church. He is the Savior of his body, the church. As the church submits to Christ, so you wives should submit to your husbands in everything.

For husbands, this means love your wives, just as Christ loved the church. He gave up his life for her to make her holy and clean, washed by the cleansing of God's word. He did this to present her to himself as a glorious church without a spot or wrinkle or any other blemish. Instead, she will be holy and without fault. In the same way, husbands ought to love their wives as they love their own bodies. For a man who loves his wife actually shows love for himself. No one hates his own body but feeds and cares for it, just as Christ cares for the church. And we are members of his body. As the Scriptures say, "A man leaves his father and mother and is joined to his wife, and the two are united into one." This is a great mystery, but it is an illustration of the way Christ and the church are one. So again I say, each man must love his wife as he loves himself, and the wife must respect her husband. (Ephesians 5:21–33)

There is no perfect marriage. At some point in a marriage, there will be an argument, disagreement, frustration, aggravation, sexual tension, and miscommunication, hopefully not all at once. Experiencing these things is not the problem. The problem is when a marriage becomes fixated or stagnated, meaning that the marriage gets struck and the couples cannot see a way out of their dilemma. So they become intoxicated with the problem and not sober with the solution. A healthy marriage is when the marriage can go through issues and come out better than before the issues arose. An unhealthy marriage is when it gets stuck, and the wheels of blame and fault-finding begin to spin continually.

Questions regarding marriage and divorce are always burning questions, extremely controversial within societies heavily influenced by Christian teaching. Opinions vary and interpretations differ. There is always the more open view that says divorce is allowed if the rift between couples is not reconciled and causes more damage than good. I do not think that couples get married in order to get divorced. However, many couples get married for the wrong reason(s): security, insecurity, way out of parents' house, 24/7 sex, career progress, more money, etc. Some couples are looking for financial security. Some people are afraid to live alone. The foundation of a marriage is very important. A brick house will endure a windstorm much better than a mobile home. Some people enter marriage like entering a mobile home. The first windstorm, the marriage will roll away. The first disagreement or argument, the couple is seeking a divorce.

Finally, fortify your marriage with the blood of Jesus, and your marriage may bend but it will not break. Make a covenant that divorce is not an option. Always remember that the grass may look greener on the other side of the fence, but in reality it is just artificial grass and it can't grow. Think with the right head and obtain all that God has for you.

SHORT
SERMONS

18

BE CAREFUL WHERE YOU LAY YOUR HEAD

Delilah realized [Samson] had finally told her the truth, so she sent for the Philistine leaders. "Come back one more time," she said, "for he has told me everything." So the Philistine leaders returned and brought the money with them. Delilah lulled Samson to sleep with his head in her lap, and she called in a man to shave off his hair, making his capture certain. And his strength left him. Then she cried out, "Samson! The Philistines have come to capture you!"

When he woke up, he thought, "I will do as before and shake myself free." But he didn't realize the LORD had left him.

So the Philistines captured him and gouged out his eyes. They took him to Gaza, where he was bound with bronze chains and made to grind grain in the prison. But before long his hair began to grow back. (Judges 16:18–22)

The Philistines were the declared enemies of God's people. Israel had strayed far from God, so He had delivered them into the hands of these enemies for forty years. God had a plan to deliver Israel. God loved Israel. So he sent his angels down to a certain couple to announce they would have a child, although the woman had been barren. God said, "He shall be a Nazarite from the day of his birth, wholly dedicated to the Lord. No razor shall come on his head, and he shall begin to deliver my people out of the hand of the Philistines."

When the child was born they named him Samson. He was blessed with great beauty and strength. As people looked at him with his long hair, they must have said, "That is God's man." Little children must have followed him. It must have been good to be his friend. It wasn't good to have been his enemy.

He was a physical giant, but a moral weakling. He mastered others, but he could not master himself.

Proverbs reminds us that a man who can rule his spirit is better than one who rules a city.

I know of people who will boast about their strong bodies and bulging muscles, but their action shows physical strength was all they had — they had no moral or spiritual power. Some people depend on their military rank for power. Some people depend on their position on their job for power. Some people depend on their looks for power. Some people depend on their money for power. Some people depend on their spouse's position for power.

The story of Samson comes down to us as an illustration of a man of great power and great beauty. He could have been a wonderful man for God, but failed the Lord because he could not control himself. Like Judas, Samson was the man who might have been.

Mike Tyson could have been one of the greatest fighters of all times. Whitney Houston could have been one of the greatest female singers of all time. Lack of self-control caused them both to fall in social status and popularity.

Strength is the first thing that comes to mind when we think of Samson. One day Samson started out to visit his girlfriend, and suddenly a lion jumped out in front of him and said to Samson, "This is my road." Samson replied with a loud and ferocious voice, "This is my road."

On another occasion, Samson thought he had been mistreated by the Philistines, so he caught 300 foxes, tied their tails together with firebrands, and scattered them into the fields of the Philistines, burning all of their crops. One night, Samson tore the gates from the hinges and carried them to a hilltop. Another time, Samson killed 1,000 Philistines with a jawbone.

Where did he get all this strength? He did not get it from his parents, nor from working out in the gym, but from God. Every time he did something great, the Spirit of the Lord came upon him.

If it had not been for God, Samson would have been like other men. When the Spirit of God comes upon you, you are able to do amazing and incredible things. Operating in the Spirit of God makes the difference between a man and a superman. It makes the difference between obedience and disobedience. It makes the difference between a true Christian and an imitation Christian.

His long hair was not the source of his strength; it was a symbol of the strength that God gave him. What is your strength?

- Playing a musical instrument
- High IQ
- Gifted singer
- Eloquent speaker
- Talented teacher
- Dynamic preacher

Your strength is not your own. It is from God. Samson took his strength for granted.

Sin will make you think that you are in love. Sin will show you the pleasure but not the pain. Sin will lead you into oppression and not liberation. Sin will give you gratification but not salvation.

Samson had many escapades and finally fell in love with a woman named Delilah, which means flirtatious.

Before Delilah, Samson had been with a prostitute. Maybe he found her on the streets, in a club, or in a bar. She was a low-class prostitute.

However, Delilah was a sophisticated prostitute. She was a high-class prostitute. She would sell out to the highest bidder.

She wrote and edited the player's handbook; she knew the book from cover to cover. Watch where you lay your head!

Sophisticated prostitutes do not hang out on street corners, or in night clubs, or in bars. They hang out in the halls of Congress, at the doors of the football draft, in NBA player rooms late at night (ask Kobe Bryant). They come to church on Sunday mornings and church conventions in the evenings, seeking a victim.

Let me elucidate the characteristics of a modern-day Delilah. They are opportunistic. They do not seek out just anybody; you have to be able to provide them something. Their motto is "nothing is for free." Delilah will get with you for a car or house payment, a diamond ring, new furniture, a job, a laptop, etc. Be careful where you lay your head. Delilah made Samson put his head in her lap, and he went to sleep.

Then, he was shorn. She had his hair cut. When you lay your head in the wrong place do not expect to wake up the same way. Samson woke up expecting to have the same power, but he did not. Furthermore, Sampson was paralyzed by his fleshly desires, which caused him to be powerless. Never underestimate the power of a woman. Samson didn't learn his lesson. His wife tricked him for the answer to the riddle.

Delilah tricked him three times before he told her the answer. Come on Samson! Wake up! Ray Charles could see this trick from the grave and brief Stevie Wonder.

But when your head is in the "lap of lust" and pleasure, you lose all sense of direction. Some laps will cause you to be blind. Some laps will cause you to have amnesia. Some laps will cause you to do wrong when you want to do right. Some laps will cause you to think that you have everything in control when you are out of control.

God gave Samson so many chances to get back on course. God will give you chances to get back on course. God chastens those He loves. . . . He loves you.

Some of us will not change. It's not that we can't, but we refuse to change. One day God will get tired of giving chances; he will give punishment. Then the consequences will be painful to bear.

Samson lost his power! As long as Samson had power, his enemies could do him no harm. When you lose your anointing and God's covering, you are powerless. When Jehovah-Shammah is no longer with you, you are prey for your enemies:

You will have no peace.

You will have no joy.

You will have no shield.

You will find yourself drowning in the pool of loneliness and despair.

You will lose your praying power.

You will lose your influence in the community.

You will lose your self-esteem.

Do not lose your power of the Holy Spirit.

The pitiful thing about Samson is that he didn't know that his strength was gone. God had departed from him.

Sometimes we continue to lay our head in the lap of Delilah and expect God to continue blessing us. We wake up expecting to have the same job position as head supervisor, expecting to have the same influence on our spouses, children, and community. We expect to sing, teach, and preach under the same anointing that we had before resting in Delilah's lap. We will not have the same power.

We drift gradually into sin, not realizing we have lost our strength, until some crisis arises, and then we realize our weaknesses.

Delilah cut Samson's hair and his pathway to life. Do not let Delilah cut your hair. Do not let Delilah take your power, peace, prayer life, position in the church, and purpose in life.

Samson lost his power. When he lost his power, the Philistines gouged his eyes out of his head. He was in total darkness. Sin will cause you to be in total darkness.

The Gospel of John reminds us that God is light, and when we break from God, we break that light. Spiritual darkness and sin are at a juxtaposition. Sin blinds us to the beauties of this world. Charles Darwin said, "When I became an agnostic I no longer saw any beauty in the flowers and the trees, and poetry and music lost its appeal to me."

The person in sin is a blinded person, blinded by Satan. Samson was imprisoned. Sin will enslave you for its purpose. Some people are in the lap of Jim Beam and Jack Daniel's, and now they are alcoholics. Some people are in the lap of anger and revenge, and now they are in prison for murder. Be careful where you lay your head!

I have good news. Samson came back to God!

But you do not have to go through what Samson went through to find God. Prisons are filled with Samsons. You do not have to go to prison in order to experience the power of God. Your strength is in the Lord Jehovah-Shammah, "the Lord is with you."

I want to close with a story that I read. Hadley Page, a famous aviator, was on a flight to Arabia in a single-person plane. As he flew along, he heard a noise that he knew was the gnawing of a large rat. As he reflected, he remembered that rats can't survive in high altitudes. So he pointed the nose of the plane upward and soared high into the clouds where it was difficult for the rat to breathe. Soon the gnawing ceased, and when he landed he found a dead rat beneath his engine.

When sin gnaws in your life, you need to rise higher into the clouds until you get closer to God. When Delilah tries to take you from the presence of God, look up and say: "Father, I stretch my hands to thee for no other help I know."

Fall on your knees and look to the hills from whence cometh your help. Your help comes from God Almighty.

Keep on climbing . . . and remember that the Lord is your light and your salvation. You shall not fear, for the Lord is the strength of your life, and of whom shall you be afraid?

19

IN THE WRONG PLACE, MESSING WITH OTHER PEOPLE'S STUFF

The following spring, the time of year when kings go to war, David sent Joab and the Israelite army to destroy the Ammonites. In the process they laid siege to the city of Rabbah. But David stayed behind in Jerusalem.

Late one afternoon David got out of bed after taking a nap and went for a stroll on the roof of the palace. As he looked out over the city, he noticed a woman of unusual beauty taking a bath. He sent someone to find out who she was, and he was told, "She is Bathsheba, the daughter of Eliam and the wife of Uriah the Hittite." Then David sent for her; and when she came to the palace, he slept with her. (She had just completed the purification rites after having her menstrual period.) Then she returned home. Later, when Bathsheba discovered that she was pregnant, she sent a message to inform David.

So David sent word to Joab: "Send me Uriah the Hittite." When Uriah arrived, David asked him how Joab and the army were getting along and how the war was progressing. Then he told Uriah, "Go on home and relax." David even sent a gift to Uriah after he had left the palace. But Uriah wouldn't go home. He stayed that night at the palace entrance with some of the king's other servants.

When David heard what Uriah had done, he summoned him and asked, "What's the matter with you? Why didn't you go home last night after being away for so long?"

Uriah replied, "The Ark and the armies of Israel and Judah are living in tents, and Joab and his officers are camping in the open fields. How could I go home to wine and dine and sleep with my wife? I swear that I will never be guilty of acting like that."

"Well, stay here tonight," David told him, "and tomorrow you may return to the army." So Uriah stayed in Jerusalem that day and the next. Then David invited him to dinner and got him drunk. But even then he couldn't get Uriah to go home to his wife. Again he slept at the palace entrance. So the next morning David wrote a letter to Joab and gave it to Uriah to deliver. The letter instructed Joab, "Station Uriah on the front lines where the battle is fiercest. Then pull back so that he will be killed." (2 Samuel 11:1-15)

God blesses the people who patiently endure testing. Afterward they will receive the crown of life that God has promised to those who love him. And remember, no one who wants to do wrong should ever say, "God is tempting me." God is never tempted to do wrong, and he never tempts anyone else either. Temptation comes from the lure of our own evil desires. These evil desires lead to evil actions, and evil actions lead to death. (James 1:12-15)

Be certain that if you are not where God wants you to be, you are destined for destruction.

Have you ever been in the wrong place, messing with other people's stuff? When you are in the wrong place, you're usually destined to do something you have no business doing.

My grandmother used to tell me, "Boy, you are some place where you have no business."

Have you ever been somewhere you were not supposed to be?

When I was in high school, we had senior skip day. It never failed, every year during "senior skip day" someone would die in a car accident, drowning, or shooting incident. Some people play hooky from work and go to various places and have affairs. They are in the wrong place, messing with other people's stuff.

David was the one God handpicked to be king of Israel. God promoted David from the pasture to the palace. When Samuel was looking for a king, he found David. David killed bears and lions. David fought and killed a giant by the name of Goliath. Saul killed his thousands, but David killed his tens of thousands.

David stayed home when he should have been fighting. The roads were clear for kings to go to battle; the weather was good. David stayed home.

God anointed David as king. When you are placed in a high position, high responsibilities come with it. God created David for that purpose. Going to war is a part of being a king. Fighting and the possibility of dying in battle is a part of it.

I have noticed in some churches that people want a leadership title, but they do not want the responsibility that comes along with the job position. They want to be a minister, but they do not want to study. They want to be a deacon, but they do not want to be a leader. They want to be the choir director, but they do not want to come to church every Sunday.

People will talk about you regardless of your good intentions. The pastor has you in office for a reason. Stay in your lane, and receive your blessings.

God has called some of you to usher and not to sing; sometimes we are so caught up in what other auxiliary leaders are doing, so we can't effectively focus on our responsibilities. Therefore, we are not where God would have us to be. Choir members should not worry about what the dance ministry is doing. Musicians should not worry about what the trustees are doing. The youth director should not worry about what the finance committee is doing.

God wants you to be where he placed you, where he called you to be. Do not stick your nose where it doesn't belong. A car battery is not concerned about what the transmission is doing. They both are going in the same direction. Lilies in the field are not concerned with the trees in the forest. Be where God called you to be. Do not call other people to see if they are going to church—you go. You say that you love the Lord— then go to church and worship him.

David stayed home! He should have been fighting in battle. A big mistake that David made was delegating his responsibility to Joab. Joab was a mighty warrior. Joab was dependable. Joab could get the job done. But there are some things you can't delegate. King David, it is time for you to fight. This is why God anointed you king.

It is not the school's job to raise your children. It is not the church's job to raise your children. It is the parents' job to raise their children. When your children are in the wrong place messing with other people's stuff, look at yourselves and not at other people.

Responsibility is yours, because God has called you. David was sleeping; he arose and walked around on the rooftop. God did not call us to sleep during the day and walk around on the rooftop. Believers have been called to go into the vineyard and work. David was in the wrong place, and he was sleeping on the job. Had David been on the battlefield fighting, he would not have been caught up with Bathsheba. It is hard to be sleeping when you are actively working. David is not the only one sleeping. God has called us to do his work for his purpose. God wants us building his kingdom, by doing outreach ministry to the lost. Some churches are only concerned with themselves. God wants us to reach out to the homeless, prostitutes, backsliders, single mothers, AIDS patients, and this broken world. Luke 4:18–19 tells us:

"The Spirit of the Lord is upon me, for he has appointed me to preach Good News to the poor. He has sent me to proclaim that captives will be released, that the blind will see, that the downtrodden will be freed from their oppressors and that the time of the Lord's favor has come."

Many churches' members are sleeping in this, the 21st century. Churches are still trying to reach people the same way they did in the 19th century. You can't expect to build church membership by preaching fire and brimstone to people Sunday after Sunday and expect the same results. You can't expect to build your youth programs by singing the same songs. You can't expect to grow spiritually when you refuse to attend Bible study. You can't expect to change mentally, when you are holding the past hostage. I am saying today, when you are not in the right place — mentally, physically, and spiritually — the devil will cause you to mess with people who are working diligently in the church. People are getting tired of messy church folks.

The devil is in the temptation business. If you are not in the right place with God, the devil will try you. The devil has tempted many religious leaders around the world, and many of the leaders have succumbed to the flesh.

Jimmy Swaggart allows the devil to take his anointed power. Jesse Jackson allows the devil to take his political power. No one is exempt from the devil's tricks and schemes. None of us can cast judgment on any of these people because all of us have done some wrong at some point in time:

Wrong place in our actions
Wrong place with our thoughts
Wrongplace with our attitudes

David was on the rooftop and saw a beautiful fine sister. He looked and saw a fine sister (36-24-36); she was built like a brick house . . . everything a man likes. She was stacked like a plate of hot buttermilk pancakes with strawberries on top. There is a little dog in all of us. Some dogs are small like poodles and some dogs are large like rotweillers.

Usually the devil will tempt us by the lust of the eyes, lust of the flesh, or pride of life. David demonstrated all three at once. When he saw Bathsheba, he allowed what he saw to give birth to sin.

One night, I was at a revival and the church was on fire (spiritual fire . . . Holy Ghost fire). A lady who was in the spirit ran around the church and passed out in front of the preachers and deacons. As she passed out, her dress flew up. The pastor jumped up and shouted, "Don't look! Don't look! The Lord will blind you!" One old deacon covered one eye and said, "The Lord might blind me, but I am going to take a chance with one eye." This goes to show that people will look regardless of the consequences. James 1:15 reminds us: "These evil desires lead to evil actions, and evil actions lead to death."

David sent the homeboys over to check her out and get the 411 — the scoop. Check it out, the Scripture tells us . . . pride before the fall. David knows that she is married because the homeboys came back and told him. He said, "I do not care." Have you been there? Knowing the right thing to do but catering to the flesh. They told him that she was married to one of his closest bodyguards (like Special Forces), your friend Uriah the Hittite. Uriah was a handpicked mercenary. He was considered to be a loyal and close friend to David. Sometimes it is your closest friend who will sleep with your spouse, girlfriend, or boyfriend. Great friendships are lost and broken over infidelity. What you do in the dark will come to the light.

Let me pause here and tell some of you to stop tell your bedroom business to your friends. Women are good for telling bedroom business, "Girl, let me tell you how he made my toes curl up. . . ." Meanwhile, your so-called friend is sitting over there thinking, "I would like to have my toes curled." Then, your friend asks the probing question, "Girl, when are you going to Florida to see your momma?" Or course, she is hoping that you leave your husband behind. . . . She is not getting that good romantic loving the way you are getting it.

When you find out that she slept with your husband, you are going to say, "How could you do this to me, I thought you were my friend?" She might tell you to stop telling your bedroom business. David walked on the rooftop, but sisters walk on rooftops as well.

Nevertheless, remember that your sins will find you out. David probably thought that he had gotten away with sleeping with Bathsheba. But she sent three words to David, "I AM PREGNANT." These three words can bring a grown man to his knees and make him holler, "Please Lord, get me out of this, don't let it be my child, give me one more chance, I will start going to church, I will preach...."

When you think that it is over, it is not over. You whisper in one another's ears, telling each other, "You are my ice cream," and, "You are my chocolate milk . . ." and nine months later you discover that you have made a milk shake. God wants you in the right place, so he can use you for his purpose.

Are you in the right place where God can use you to lead people to Christ?

Let me tell you, sin leads to more sin. Sin has the strongest shovel in the world; sin will keep on digging and digging, until you are buried in sin, shame, and guilt.

David tried to cover up his sins by bringing Uriah from the war to sleep with his wife: Uriah said, "I can't sleep with my wife when my troops are on the battlefield." David tried and tried! What do you do when your lie does not work? David had Uriah killed. Had David been in the war, fighting and leading his troops, he would not have been in this situation.

We get mad at people for working in the church—doing what we should be doing—so we talk about them, and when that does not work, we kill them; we assassinate their character and lifestyle.

Nevertheless, God forgave David. David still had to deal with the consequences: his first son died, and his household fell into anarchy.

There is good news. If you seek God, he will renew in you a right spirit.

Maybe you have fallen into sin, and maybe you are in the wrong place, but God is waiting for you to get in the right place. God is waiting to forgive you. Isaiah 43:25 tells us that "I am he who blots out your transgressions, for my own sake, and remembers your sins no more."

In 2 Samuel 12, Nathan brings David face-to-face with his sins. Only when you face your sins can you begin the healing, forgiving, and reconciliation process. When you come face-to-face with your sins, then you can see sin for what it is—death.

Scripture says: "The wages of sin is death, but the gift of God is eternal life in Christ Jesus our Lord" (Romans 6:23).

Psalm 51:1–3, 6–14

Have mercy on me, O God,
because of your unfailing love.
Because of your great compassion,
blot out the stain of my sins.
Wash me clean from my guilt.
[I know of a washing detergent that is greater than, Tide, Surf, Ajax, or Gain. The detergent that I am talking about is nothing but the blood of Jesus.]
For I recognize my shameful deeds . . . .
But you desire honesty from the heart,
so you can teach me to be wise in my inmost being.
Purify me from my sins, and I will be clean;
wash me, and I will be whiter than snow.
Oh, give me back my joy again;
Remove the stain of my guilt.

Create in me a clean heart, O God.
Renew a right spirit within me.
Do not banish me from your presence,
and do not take your Holy Spirit from me.
Restore to me again the joy of your salvation,
and make me willing to obey you.
Then I will teach your ways to sinners,
and they will return to you.
Forgive me for shedding blood, O God who saves;
then I will joyfully sing of your forgiveness.